A PLANTSMAN'S GUIDE TO

RHODODENDRONS

KENNETH COX

A PLANTSMAN'S GUIDE TO
RHODODENDRONS

KENNETH COX

SERIES EDITOR
ALAN TOOGOOD

WARD LOCK

DEDICATION

To my father and grandfather, for obvious
reasons.

First published in Great Britain in 1989
by Ward Lock Limited, Artillery House,
Artillery Row, London SW1P 1RT, a
Cassell Company

House editor Denis Ingram

Text filmset in Times Roman
by Dorchester Typesetting Group Ltd

Printed by BPCC Hazell Books Ltd,
Member of BPCC Ltd, Aylesbury, Bucks, England

British Library Cataloguing in Publication Data

Cox, Kenneth
    A plantsman's guide to rhododendrons.
    1. Gardens. Rhododendrons
    I. Title   II. Series
    635.9'3362

ISBN 0-7063-6754-5

CONTENTS

PUBLISHER'S NOTE

Readers are requested to note that in order to make the text intelligible in both hemispheres, plant flowering times, etc. are described in terms of seasons, not months. The following table provides an approximate 'translation' of seasons into months for the two hemispheres.

Northern Hemisphere		Southern Hemisphere
Mid-winter	= January	= Mid-summer
Late winter	= February	= Late summer
Early spring	= March	= Early autumn
Mid-spring	= April	= Mid-autumn
Late spring	= May	= Late autumn
Early summer	= June	= Early winter
Mid-summer	= July	= Mid-winter
Late summer	= August	= Late winter
Early autumn	= September	= Early spring
Mid-autumn	= October	= Mid-spring
Late autumn	= November	= Late spring
Early winter	= December	= Early summer

Captions for colour photographs on chapter-opening pages:

Pp. 8-9 Deciduous azaleas, hardy hybrids and polyanthus provide spectacular colour in Golder's Hill Park, North London.

Pp. 18-19 The Japanese azalea 'Hatsuguri' rarely fails to give a spectacular display.

Pp. 42-43 One of the finest large-leaved species, *R. macabeanum*, with large trusses of yellow flowers.

Pp. 86-87 'Fantastica', an exiting new German *yakushimanum* hybrid, sure to become popular.

Pp. 112-113 Massed displays of deciduous azaleas in an informal woodland setting.

Pp. 122-123 Azalea 'Gibraltar', one of the most widely grown of the Knaphill/Exbury deciduous azalea hybrids.

EDITOR'S FOREWORD

This unique series takes a completely fresh look at the most popular garden and greenhouse plants.

Written by a team of leading specialists, yet suitable for novice and more experienced gardener alike, the series considers modern uses of the plants, including refreshing ideas for combining them with other garden or greenhouse plants. This should appeal to the more general gardener who, unlike the specialist, does not want to devote a large part of the garden to a particular plant. Many of the planting schemes and modern uses are beautifully illustrated in colour.

The extensive A-Z lists describe in great detail hundreds of the best hybrids and species available today.

For the historically-minded, each book opens with a brief history of the subject up to the present day and, as appropriate, looks at the developments by plant breeders.

The books cover all you need to know about growing and propagating. The former embraces such aspects as suitable sites and soils, planting methods, all-year-round care and how to combat pests, diseases and disorders.

Propagation includes raising plants from seeds and by vegetative means, as appropriate.

For each subject there is a society (sometimes more than one), full details of which round-off each book.

The plants that make up this series are very popular and examples can be found in many gardens. However, it is hoped that these books will also encourage gardeners to try some of the more unusual varieties; ensure some stunning plant associations; and result in the plants being grown well.

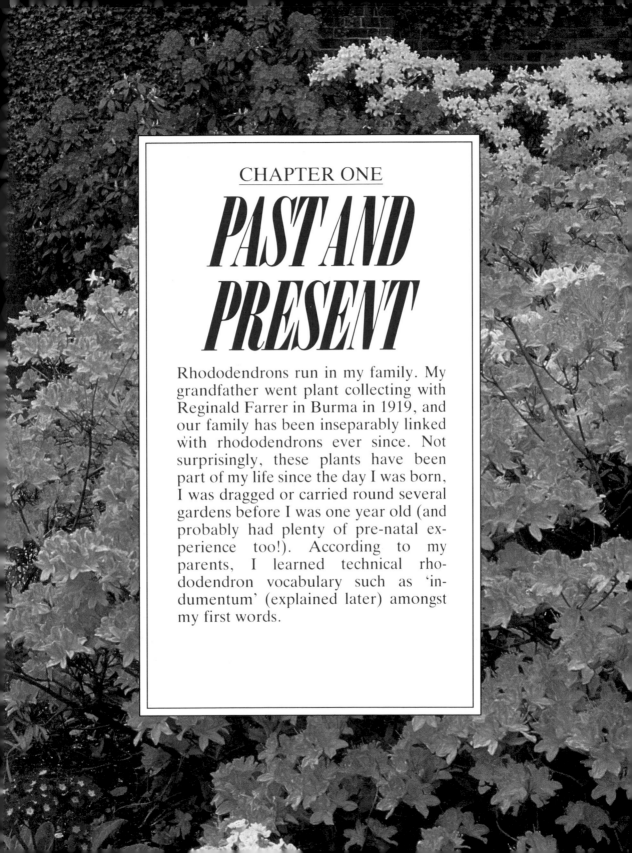

CHAPTER ONE

PAST AND PRESENT

Rhododendrons run in my family. My grandfather went plant collecting with Reginald Farrer in Burma in 1919, and our family has been inseparably linked with rhododendrons ever since. Not surprisingly, these plants have been part of my life since the day I was born, I was dragged or carried round several gardens before I was one year old (and probably had plenty of pre-natal experience too!). According to my parents, I learned technical rhododendron vocabulary such as 'indumentum' (explained later) amongst my first words.

SO, CAN ANYONE GROW RHODODENDRONS?

Rhododendrons are such diverse plants from such an extraordinary range of climates that there are few parts of the world where at least one or two varieties cannot be grown. Rhododendron species from tropical climates such as the forests of Papua New Guinea enjoy climates of high temperatures and high humidity, while the high-altitude and more northern species can tolerate winter lows as cold as $-32°C$ ($-25°F$).

Ideal climates for rhododendrons are found in much of continental Europe, the British Isles, North America, Australia and New Zealand, as well as in the rhododendron heartlands of Asia. In severe climates, where excess heat, sun or cold are encountered, forms of artificial protection can be used to permit rhododendron cultivation. Many rhododendrons make fine indoor plants for the greenhouse or conservatory, while there are few countries where Japanese azaleas are not grown as successful pot-plants.

Wherever you live, it is probably worth trying to grow these magnificent plants. They give an unrivalled display in flower, and provide so many thousands of gardeners with hours of pleasure.

Recent victims of the rhododendron bug should be warned of the addiction which these plants cause. Once discovered, no other plants seem to provide quite the same impact or interest. Perhaps rose, dahlia and chrysanthemum growers show a similar intensity of enthusiasm (and sometimes narrow-mindedness) for a single genus, but these are surely people who have not discovered rhododendrons (or who are condemned to a life on alkaline soil)! Interest in rhododendrons can range from the casual admiration of their beauty, to the species fanatic who would go anywhere, pay anything and probably kill in order to get a plant of that obscure, rare, shy-flowering species with an unpronounceable name. Whatever form your interest in rhododendrons takes, I'm sure they can provide you with much satisfaction and pleasure.

To many people, the word 'rhododendron' is synonymous with a large, dense bush with rather uninteresting green leaves, which covers itself in pink, red, lavender or white flowers in late spring or early summer. While some rhododendrons do indeed fit this stereotype, it is far from being the whole picture. The genus *Rhododendron* is in fact one of the largest in the plant kingdom, including more than 800 distinct species from four continents. These range from giant forest trees up to 24m (80ft) high to tiny alpines which creep along the ground, while the leaf size ranges from 5mm–1m ($\frac{1}{4}$in–$3\frac{1}{4}$ft) in length.

Rhododendron species have flowers of almost every colour imaginable, in many shapes and sizes; deep reds, pale pinks, creams, yellows, pure whites, rich purples and combinations of these. Some flowers are spotted, while others have a bold flare in the throat, giving a two-toned effect. Rhododendrons hold their flowers in groups called trusses and these can be full, tall and cone-shaped, or loose and informal. Some trusses have over 30 flowers in them, others have only one or two.

In addition, rhododendrons often have very fine foliage, which can obviously add to their year-round ornamental appeal. Many species are grown as much for the leaves as the flowers, and the keenest rhododendron collectors are usually fanatical foliage enthusiasts. Very few, if any other, evergreen plants offer such a striking combination of attractive foliage and spectacular flowers.

Azaleas also form part of the genus *Rhododendron*. These take many forms, from the evergreen ones commonly sold as houseplants in the U.K. to the bright yellows, oranges and reds of the Exbury and Knaphill deciduous azalea hybrids. These hybrid groups were raised from azalea species from places as far apart as Turkey, China, Japan, Taiwan and North America.

In recent years, rhododendrons have had rather a bad press, due to publicity concerning the lavender-pink 'wild' *Rhododendron ponticum*. This species is an invasive pest in many southern and western parts of the U.K., and new plantings of it are quite rightly banned in some areas. The sins of *R. ponticum* have to some extent been visited on the whole genus, causing a general prejudice for all rhododendrons. This is entirely unjustified, as it is only *R. ponticum* which causes any problems. No other species or hybrids pose any threat to the environment, and the innocence of 99% of all rhododendron varieties should be vigorously proclaimed.

WHERE DO RHODODENDRONS COME FROM?

Several rhododendron species are native to Europe. The aforementioned *R. ponticum* comes from parts of Turkey, Lebanon, Spain and Portugal. *R. luteum*, the well-known sweetly-scented yellow azalea species, also comes from Turkey, and its distribution spreads north as far as Poland and the Soviet Union. The first species to be introduced to Britain was *R. hirsutum*, a form of the well-known Alpenrose which, with its close relation *R. ferrugineum*, is found in many parts of the Austrian and Swiss Alps, the Yugoslavian Dolomites and also in the Pyrenees. Another species, *R. lapponicum*, has a circumpolar distribution in northern Europe, Siberia, Alaska and Greenland. North America boasts several rhododendron species, and among these are featured some of the deciduous azaleas which were used as the parents of the Knaphill/Exbury hybrids, and *R. catawbiense*, one of the hardiest of all species, used extensively by hybridizers to breed the so-called 'hardy hybrids'.

These species represent just the outer fringes of the total distribution of rhododendrons which finds its centre in Asia, in the Himalayan countries such as Nepal, Bhutan and Burma' and in south-west China. Some species are found in almost every Asian country from Siberia to Malaya and Indonesia, and from Afghanistan to Korea, Japan

(Opposite) R. campylocarpum *taken in the wild in Nepal at approximately 3100 m (10,500 ft).*

and Taiwan. At lower elevations, rhododendrons often grow as large forest trees, sometimes forming the dominant vegetation over wide areas. *R. arboreum* forests, for instance, produce a blaze of red flowers in the spring in Nepal and northern India though, alas, many *arboreum*-covered hillsides are being cut down. Higher up the mountain sides, the rhododendrons become smaller, hardier and more compact, growing as dense, mounded or tangled shrubs among coniferous forest. Above the tree-line, the dwarf alpine types are found which grow as twiggy, small-leaved bushes often growing like carpets over whole hillsides, like Himalayan heather.

□ PLANT COLLECTORS

Most of the Asiatic species were discovered and introduced by Western plant-collectors during the period 1840–1949. Some of the early collectors were missionaries who were the first Europeans to venture into the areas where the plants were found. Later, nurseries, such as Veitch in England, and botanic institutions, such as Kew Gardens and the Arnold Arboretum in the U.S.A., financed professional plant-collectors, such as Ernest Wilson, George Forrest and Frank Kingdon-Ward, to mount long and thorough collecting expeditions. Plants were discovered, specimens were pressed and seed was collected, and these were sent back by sea to Kew, Edinburgh, Boston and elsewhere for identification. These explorers and others introduced thousands of plants to the West, including many of our commonest garden plants. As well as rhododendrons, these men and others were the first collectors of many camellias, magnolias, berberis, primulas, gentians and other kinds of trees and shrubs. The names of many of these plants reflect their collectors; *Magnolia wilsonii, Primula forrestii* and *Rhododendron wardii* are some examples.

It was certainly no package holiday for the early collectors, whose work was long, arduous and often dangerous. George Forrest and Reginald Farrer died during expeditions. Robert Fortune had to repel pirates while travelling in a junk off the Chinese coast, while the unfortunate French missionary Père Soulié (who discovered *Rhododendron souliei* and *Buddleia davidii*) was tortured and shot by Tibetan monks. The stories of the plant-hunters are told in the books they wrote between trips; many are well worth reading. By the outbreak of the Second World War, due to political upheavals and understandable suspicions of all things Western, many of the Asian countries had closed their borders to Westerners, cutting off the source of new plant introductions. Happily, in recent times most have re-opened to tourists to some extent, although many are not keen on people collecting plant materials. The records of the great collectors indicated that there were many rhododendron species and other plants which had never reached the West, but recent European

'Jean Marie de Montague', a popular bright red, medium-sized hybrid, which is widely available.

and American expeditions have managed to introduce some of them. Chinese botanists are now hard at work discovering and classifying more new plants; hopefully some of these will also reach Western gardens over the next few years.

In Malaya and Indonesia another group of rhododendrons called the 'Vireyas' is found. These often have stunning flowers in bright colours of many shades. Many of these plants are epiphytic (i.e. they grow on other plants), hanging down amongst the trees of the tropical rainforest. As might be imagined from their native habitat, these species are tender, needing green-

house cultivation in northern Europe. There was a craze for them in Victorian times, coinciding with the great age of the glasshouse and conservatory, but now they are rarely seen outside botanic gardens and specialist collections. They can be grown outside in parts of Australia, New Zealand, California and elsewhere, where the heat, humidity and lack of frosts imitate their native climate.

It is the American and Himalayan species which lend themselves best to widespread garden cultivation, due to the fact that the climate of a mountain in say, Nepal, at 3000–4000 m (10,000–13,000 ft) is surprisingly comparable to that of densely populated lowland areas in several parts of the western world. Most of the Asian rhododendrons come from areas in the wet monsoon mountain zone. Although relatively near the equator, the high altitude and prevalence of high rainfall, mist, damp and winter snow, give rhododendrons ideal growing conditions. Amongst those areas where the climate is comparable to the monsoon mountain zone are the u.k. and Ireland, parts of Europe with a maritime climate, coastal North America, Chile, New Zealand and parts of Australia and Japan.

Rhododendron species vary greatly in hardiness depending on the location and altitude of collection in the wild. Species from, say, Sichuan province in China, are usually hardier than species found further south, in northern India for instance. Species from high altitudes are usually hardier than those from further down the mountainside or in the valleys below. Often a single species is found over a wide area (sometimes in several countries), showing a great variation in hardiness, flower colour, foliage, etc. Collectors generally aim to introduce plants from the highest possible altitude to ensure survival outdoors in colder gardens. They also search for forms with the best flowers and/or most spectacular foliage.

HYBRIDIZING

As far as garden potential is concerned, species rhododendrons form only part of the story. As with most types of ornamental plant, man has been tampering with nature, enthusiastically raising hybrids which can in some way offer something unavailable among species. From the time early last century when the first American and Asiatic species were introduced into Europe, hybridizers have been raising hundreds of new named hybrid rhododendrons and azaleas. Over 10 000 have been registered with the Royal Horticultural Society, and all over the world professionals and amateurs make crosses every spring, hoping for something even better.

The first important hybridizing breakthroughs early last century led to the breeding of the so-called 'hardy hybrids'. These are the large bushes with pink, lavender and reddish flowers which form most people's conception of what a rhododendron should look like, and they are still perhaps the most important group of rhododendrons for general planting. The most rugged of these hybrids are known as the 'ironclads'. Hardy to at least −29°C (−20°F), this group provides the majority of rhododendrons suitable for really severe climates. 'Roseum Elegans', 'P.J.M.' and 'Nova Zembla' are amongst the most common ironclad rhododendrons.

Japanese or evergreen azalea hybridizing is, however, a much older activity. The Japanese have been collecting, selecting and crossing their native azaleas, and using them in their formal gardens, often using bonsai techniques, for hundreds of years. Dutch merchants

R. decorum, *one of the easiest and hardiest scented species to grow. Useful for its drought tolerance.*

'Naomi'. There are several named clones of this fragrant hybrid raised at Exbury Gardens near Southampton.

discovered these hybrids in the 18th century, and Robert Fortune introduced the first one into Britain in 1844. Surprisingly, the garden potential of these azaleas was not realized until early this century, when the famous Dutch nursery firms of Van Nes and Koster began to promote them. Many of the Japanese azaleas were introduced to Britain and the U.S.A. by the collector Ernest Wilson, and these azaleas, together with several other species from Japan, Taiwan, India and elsewhere, have been used in extensive breeding programmes (which still continue today) to produce both the azaleas seen as houseplants, and the outdoor 'evergreen' or 'Japanese' ones which produce the familiar red, pink and white flowers.

As plant collectors discovered and introduced more and more new rho-

dodendron species during the early part of this century, the palette of colours and shapes for hybridizing became larger and larger. Rich English aristocrats such as Lionel de Rothschild and Lord Aberconway instigated breeding programmes with the new species as soon as they first flowered, competing for awards at London shows. The scale of Lionel de Rothschild's breeding was awesome: over a million seedlings were raised by a staff which topped a hundred at times. The resulting hybrids such as 'Naomi', 'Carita' and 'Crest' are still amongst the finest available, and are grown all over the world.

Dutch and German nurseries, with more modest breeding programmes, produced fine commercial hybrids such as 'Britannia' and 'Jean Marie de Montague', while in eastern U.S.A., the industrialist Charles Dexter and the nurseryman Joe Gable began crossing hardy hybrids with new Himalayan species. Azaleas also caught the attention of hybridizers. By crossing and recrossing the Asian and American species and the earlier hybrids, the familiar Knaphill and Exbury hybrids were produced.

Since the Second World War, North America has emerged as the most important contributor to hybridizing; hundreds of professional nurserymen and amateur enthusiasts have evolved complex breeding programmes, and many of their hybrids can be found described in Chapter 3. Other important hybrids are being raised at the present time in West Germany, Australia, New Zealand and Japan, as well as some in Britain.

Many hybrids are now very complex, with up to 20 different species involved in their parentage, and the diverse climatic conditions in different regions have required breeders to try to produce new hybrids with extreme cold tolerance, heat and sun tolerance, disease resistance and other characteristics. The result of all this activity is that every year many new hybrids are released, and usually some of them are good enough to become popular. Hybridizing is a slow process, requiring a great deal of patience; few rhododendrons flower at an age of less than five years from seed, and sorting out and testing the best offspring takes a lot longer. Some people claim that less than one in a hundred crosses made will produce really good results, but it could be argued this depends on the skill of the hybridizer and the complexity of the goals being sought.

Wherever rhododendrons can be grown well, there should be a considerable range of suitable varieties from which to choose. There are literally hundreds of species and hybrids available for most areas, and choosing which ones to grow can be a daunting prospect when faced with a huge catalogue of names. The species and hybrids described in Chapter 3 of this book give a selection of around two hundred of the best of these, but many others will probably be available and popular in your area. Local nurserymen and garden centres should be able to provide helpful advice for selecting the varieties most suitable for local climatic conditions. Better still, join your local rhododendron society and make use of the expertise of its members.

CHAPTER TWO

PLANTING IDEAS

Rhododendrons and azaleas are versatile plants which can thrive in a variety of situations, provided certain conditions are met (see Chapter 4 for details of cultural requirements). Rhododendrons belong to the family *Ericaceae* (or heath family). In addition to heathers, and rhododendrons and azaleas, this family includes *Andromeda*, *Enkianthus*, *Gaultheria*, *Kalmia*, *Pernettya* and others. The unifying features of all these plants is their requirement of acid soil and their compact, shallow, fibrous root systems.

If there is one single piece of advice for the successful garden planting of rhododendrons, it is to plant them in groups. There are several reasons for this.

The fibrous rootball of rhododendrons needs fairly constant moisture in the growing season, and competition from other plants with deeper, greedier or shallower roots usually prevents them from getting the water they need. In addition, in a clump rhododendrons can shade one another's roots and, once the plants in a clump join up, can prevent weeds growing over the roots. The leaf drop from a group of rhododendrons becomes an ideal mulch for the roots beneath, holding in moisture and keeping the soil cool in summer and insulated in winter. Most rhododendrons are social plants in the wild where they grow in colonies, sometimes of hundreds of plants, protecting one another, and this should be imitated wherever possible in the garden.

One common mistake is to plant rhododendrons individually in holes made in lawns. Almost invariably, the grass grows over the rootball, starving it of moisture, causing the rhododendron to languish. If you do want to plant rhododendrons on lawns, plant a clump of three or more in a bed, and keep an area around the roots free of grass and weeds. For the reasons outlined above, I would recommend that, if you want to grow more than one or two rhododendrons in your garden, you do not dot them around, but plant them together. This usually provides a better visual effect and produces healthier plants. Informality is the key to attractive rhododendron plantings. Straight-edged beds and grid planting just don't suit their form. Rhododendrons generally cannot be pruned into shape without the loss of flower buds, so making the best use of their natural growth habit is the best tactic.

FLOWERING PERIODS

Although the peak of rhododendron flowering is in late spring and early summer, there are rhododendrons which flower very early or very late in the season, providing a potential flowering period in milder and moderate areas of up to nine months of the year. In colder gardens the flowering season is compressed, starting considerably later. Deep in winter, sometimes even before Christmas in the U.K., the hybrid 'Nobleanum', and the species *R. dauricum* 'Midwinter' open their flowers. The flowers of the latter can withstand several degrees of frost. From this time onwards, there is a succession of suitable species and hybrids to give a range of colour right through until late summer. A few rhododendrons have frost-hardy flowers, but most will lose their flowers to frost once the buds have begun to swell. Most gardens have mild periods during some part of the early spring, allowing some early flowerers to open. Unless you have a garden which has such persistent and regular late frosts that you virtually never have good early flowering, it is definitely well worth growing a selection of early flowering rhododendrons. At the time of writing at Glendoick in early February 1989, we actually have 70 different rhododendrons in flower due to the exceptionally mild weather.

□ A SELECTION OF EARLY-FLOWERING RHODODENDRONS

R. barbatum – red
R. calophytum – pink/white
R. dauricum – purple/white
R. oreodoxa – pink
R. mucronulatum – pink
R. vernicosum – pink
'Bo Peep' – yellow
'Christmas Cheer' – pink
'Cilpinense' – pink/white
'Nobleanum' – red/pink/white
'Praecox' – rosy purple
'Ptarmigan' – white
'Snow Lady' – white

Having the flowers frosted should not harm the plant in any way, but a plant which never has a chance to flower properly is obviously better replaced by something later and hardier.

At the other end of the flowering season are the late species and hybrids flowering from midsummer onwards. As a general rule, these tend to be rather tall and rangy, best in sheltered and shaded sites. Some examples include the species *R. auriculatum* and *R. griersonianum* and the hybrids 'Polar Bear' and 'Azor'. Some deciduous azaleas such as *R. occidentale* also flower late in the season, and these will tolerate more exposed sites than the midsummer rhododendrons.

R. yakushimanum. *A very beautiful species suitable for the smaller garden. The parent of hundreds of 'yak' hybrids.*

FOLIAGE

It is not just the flowers which attract gardeners to rhododendrons; they have amongst the most spectacular and varied foliage of all evergreens, especially during the time when the new growth unfurls. The importance of attractive foliage to a planting of rhododendrons is obvious, as it is this which provides the visual stimulus for most of the year. Leaf size from tiny to 1 m (3¼ ft) provides plenty of contrasts, as does the variety of leaf shapes. From the round leaves of *R. orbiculare* to the pointed ones of *R. roxieanum*, from the giant leaves of *R. sinogrande* to the tiny *R. keleticum* Radicans Gp. The leaves of *R. edgeworthii* are matt and rough in texture, while those of *R. wardii* and *R. williamsianum* are smooth. The glaucous-blue leaves of *R. campanulatum* ssp. *aeruginosum* or *R. fastigiatum*, or the purple and bronze winter foliage of 'P.J.M.' and related hybrids, provide fine contrasts.

Many species of rhododendron, and a few hybrids, have a covering of small hairs called indumentum on the leaves, usually on the underside, but sometimes above too, or on the stems. This usually forms a fur, skin or felt-like layer which can be deep brown, rufous, silvery, fawn, or white. Many people are surprised when they first notice this, and some even fear that it is a disease, but indumentum is probably the attribute most prized by the rhododendron connoisseur. You can always recognize a rhodoholic in a garden, as he or she will be forever turning over the leaves of rhododendrons looking for indumentum. Hybrids of the Japanese species *R. yakushimanum* are perhaps the most widely-grown example of rhododendrons with indumentum. Indumented species are especially attractive as the new growth unfurls, because the leaf undersides point outwards, and the usually white or brown, downy hairs make a spectacular show, sometimes as good as a second flowering. Among the most striking indumented species are *R. yakushimanum*, *R. bureavii* and *R. falconeri* ssp. *eximium*.

□ SOME EXAMPLES OF ATTRACTIVE LEAVES IN RHODODENDRONS

Rounded leaves – *R. campylocarpum*, *R. orbiculare*, *R. souliei*, *R. thomsonii*, *R. williamsianum*, 'Bow Bells', 'Linda', 'Moonstone'.

Blue leaves – *R. campanulatum* ssp. *aeruginosum*, *R. fastigiatum*, *R. lepidostylum*, *R. mekongense* Viridescens Gp., *R. oreotrephes*, *R. thomsonii*, 'Intrifast'.

Indumented leaves – *R. bureavii*, *R. falconeri* ssp. *eximium*, *R. pachysanthum*, *R. tsariense*, 'Ken Janeck', 'Sir Charles Lemon'.

At certain times of the year, some rhododendrons offer striking colour effects from their leaves and young growth. *R. lutescens* has reddish new growth, while that of *R. williamsianum* and its hybrids is usually brown. Species such as *R. auriculatum*, and hybrids

'Praecox'. A widely grown, tough, early flowering hybrid.

such as 'Loderi', have bright red leaf bracts which cover the young leaves and unfurl like candles in the early summer. 'Elizabeth Lockhart' has purple leaves which remain purple all the year round if grown in shade. A few species have particularly attractive bark, sometimes smooth, sometimes peeling, in colours ranging from pink, deep red and purple to silvery and grey. *R. thomsonii*, *R. barbatum*, and *R. hodgsonii* are some examples. Some species take a very long time to flower and are grown almost entirely for their foliage. One species sought by collectors is *R. pronum* which has fine blue-green leaves. It was introduced during the 1930s, and has only flowered about twice in cultivation in the intervening 50 years. Luckily this species is the exception and not the rule, otherwise we'd be planting for future generations to see any flowers!

SCENT

Some rhododendrons have the additional attribute of scent. Most of the scented types have flowers of the paler colours, white, pale pink and pale lavender. Some of the scented species and hybrids are rather tender, only suitable for greenhouse or conservatory, unless you live in a mild area without severe frosts. If you keep these tender species in containers, they can be brought into the house in flower for the best appreciation of their scent. There are, however, several much hardier species and hybrids which also provide fine scent. Most of these relate to the Fortunea subsection (rhododendron species are

□ **RHODODENDRONS FOR SCENT**

H5 very hardy, H4 hardy, H3 average, H2/1 tender

R. auriculatum H5
R. decorum H4
R. edgeworthii H2–3
R. fortunei H5
R. griffithianum H2–3
R. lindleyi H2-3
R. luteum H4–5
R. maddenii H2–3
R. occidentale H4
'Fragrantissimum' H2
'Lady Alice Fitzwilliam' H2–3
'Lavender Girl' H5
'Loderi' H3–4
'Naomi' H4–5
'Polar Bear' H4
+ many deciduous azalea hybrids

classified into groups called subsections), including *R. fortunei* and *R. decorum*. Many hybrids have been raised from these, the most famous being the magnificent 'Loderi'. Scent is also to be found in many deciduous azaleas. There are no scented red rhododendrons.

Stimulation for the nose also comes from the foliage of some species. *R. anthopogon* leaves are used as incense in Nepal, and species such as *R. rubiginosum* and *R. glaucophyllum* have leaves with a striking aroma.

COMPANION PLANTS

Many books concentrate quite heavily on which plants should and should not be grown with rhododendrons. In reality, this is largely a matter of personal taste, and of adapting to the available garden situation, i.e. whether you have an open or woodland site, whether it covers 10 acres or half an acre. Some people, for instance, like the mixture of dwarf conifers and dwarf rhododendrons, while others abhor it, and the same diversity of opinion is true of almost all combinations. When considering companion plants, there is really only one golden rule: to bring out the best in your rhododendrons, other plants must not compete directly with the rhododendron roots. The shallow, compact fibrous roots of rhododendrons need to have free access to as much of the soil's moisture as possible, and if the roots of other greedy plants are allowed to run near, over, or under the rhododendrons, the rhododendrons will usually suffer. With this in mind, you can plant whatever you like to complement them.

The most obvious companion plants for rhododendrons are others of the family *Ericaceae* (heath family) to which rhododendrons belong. Heathers themselves are very greedy as regards moisture consumption, and should not be planted among rhododendrons. By all means plant heathers in a group in the same bed, at the front for instance, as they do make a fine contrast in flower and foliage, and they can extend the flowering season in the summer and autumn, after the rhododendrons have finished. In peat gardens with dwarf rhododendrons, try *Andromeda, Cassiope, Phyllodoce*, and dwarf *Gaulther-*

ia, Kalmia, Menziesia, and *Vaccinium*. In the woodland garden larger ericaceous plants such as *Arbutus, Enkianthus* and *Pieris* are ideal.

Camellias enjoy similar conditions to rhododendrons and they are amongst the best companions for them. Asiatic meconopsis, primulas and incarvilleas, which often associate with rhododendrons in the wild, and trilliums, erythroniums, and many similar plants, make fine companion plants but again, plant them in groups, rather than scattered singly through the rhododendrons. Many fine colour combinations can be made between companion plants and rhododendrons. *R. dauricum* 'Midwinter' has purple flowers which contrast well with yellow and cream hamamelis for very early colour, while the whites and pinks of flowering cherries can show off the yellow-flowered rhododendrons. Red-leaved and variegated *Acer palmatum* cultivars make a fine foil for rhododendron foliage. The potential for such contrasts is infinite; many will be fortuitously made in the general course of planting.

□ LATE SUMMER AND WINTER

In a planting which is predominantly of rhododendrons, it is inevitable that there will be a lack of colour in late summer and winter. Viburnums, eucryphias, buddleias, hydrangeas and many other shrubs can be planted to remedy this. Many daphnes bloom at lean times of the year for rhododendron flowers, and most enjoy similar conditions to rhododendrons. In addition to the autumn colour of deciduous azaleas, that

R. augustinii, *one of the nearest to true 'blue' rhododendron species. Not for very cold gardens.*

of acers and other deciduous trees looks especially striking set off against the evergreen leaves of rhododendrons. Many berrying shrubs such as pernettyas, berberis and pyracanthas, and trees such as malus and sorbus can also provide fine autumn colours. Deep in winter, hamamelis, winter-flowering viburnums and mahonia provide fine contrast for the earliest flowering rhododendrons.

Groups of rhododendrons can be interplanted with herbaceous perennials to give colour later in the season, but beware of rampant plants which cannot be kept in bounds; if they run around over the rhododendron roots the rhododendrons will suffer. It also makes sense to use plants which like similar soil conditions and moisture. Some good examples include *Astilbe, Bergenia, Epimedium, Hemerocallis, Hosta, Polygonum affine* and *Thalictrum*. In a woodland garden underplanting with bluebells, snowdrops, aconites, ferns, foxgloves and other plants can give added interest without adversely affecting the rhododendrons. These are just some of the many combinations which are possible. As outlined previously, as long as the roots of your companion plants do not adversely affect the rhododendrons, almost any plants should be useful for creative and attractive garden display.

'Elizabeth', one of the best low red hybrids, planted to contrast with the white tree heath Erica veitchii.

Rhododendrons can be divided into five or six main groups as far as their use in gardens is concerned, each having several specific attributes.

DWARFS

For a small town garden, the dwarf rhododendrons are perhaps the best choice, in that even in the smallest area, quite a large collection can be grown. While the individual flowers are not as large or as spectacular as, say, the hardy hybrids, the overall effect is often just as showy, as most dwarf rhododendrons

are extremely free flowering, so much so that the foliage is often completely hidden. Most hardy dwarfs come from high altitudes in the Himalayas and elsewhere, and this high altitude is reflected in their smaller leaves which can stand full exposure. In a garden, dwarf species and hybrids should generally be planted in an open situation, in groups so that they can grow together forming a carpet or mat. Place the taller growing varieties in the back of a bed, with the smaller ones at the front. Dwarfs range from creepers such as *R. keleticum* and *R. forrestii* Repens Gp., neat fastigiate plants like 'Anna Baldsiefen', to rounded or mounding shrubs such as 'Whisperingrose', *R. williamsianum* and 'Scarlet Wonder'. Using this variety of growth habits, interesting effects can be created.

One recent development amongst smaller rhododendrons are the 'yak' hybrids derived from the Japanese species *R. yakushimanum*. This species passes on its neat habit, free flowering, hardiness and full trusses to its offspring, and its hundreds of hybrids, bred all over the world, provide a range of colours on compact plants suitable for smaller gardens. This allows the type of full rounded truss seen in the larger hybrids to be carried on hybrids of smaller stature. These can be thoroughly recommended for all sizes of gardens.

□ 'YAK' HYBRIDS

Red	– 'Dopey', 'Titian Beauty'
Pink	– 'Bashful', 'Hydon Dawn', 'Morgenrot', 'Pink Cherub'
Yellow	– 'Golden Torch'
Cream	– 'Grumpy'
Lavender	– 'Caroline Allbrook', 'Hoppy', 'Sleepy'
Peach	– 'Percy Wiseman'
White	– 'Seven Stars'
Two-tone	– 'Fantastica', 'Surrey Heath'

□ PLANTING

Planting rhododendrons in a rock garden can be very successful. In areas of high rainfall, a rock garden will often provide the planting sites with the best drainage, and it is even possible to plant on top of mossy rocks. In drier rock gardens, perfect for many alpine plants,

the soil will probably be too dry for rhododendrons. In this case it is best to select an area specifically for the rhododendrons and add plenty of organic matter to allow sufficient moisture retention. In the wild, many dwarfs grow in the lee of rocks to gain moisture, to maintain cool roots and to give a degree of wind protection, and this can be imitated in the rock garden.

In a larger garden, if space permits, it is worth planting dwarfs in groups of three or more for a bolder effect. If you plant singly, be careful to place plants of similar vigour next to each other to avoid the stronger growers swamping the more compact ones. One or two dwarf rhododendrons flower in mid and late winter but the peak of flowering is in early spring. Many fine colour contrasts can be made, one of the most effective being the blues and purples of *R. russatum* , *R. fastigiatum* and 'Blue Diamond' with the yellows of 'Chikor', 'Curlew', 'Patty Bee', etc. The foliage textures of beds of dwarfs, especially those with grey or blue leaves like *R. fastigiatum* and *R. calostrotum* 'Gigha' can give an attractive year-round effect, as can the indumented leaves of *R. yakushimanum* and its hybrids.

□ PEAT BED

Another common way of growing dwarfs is as part of a peat bed. This is made up with a very high percentage of peat in imitation of moorland soil. This must be well drained, and some bark may be added to the medium to achieve this. Such peat beds are suitable for most dwarf rhododendrons as well as

'Dopey', a fine red-flowered 'yak' hybrid suitable for the smaller garden.

dwarf *Ericaceae* such as cassiopes and phyllodoces, primulas, trilliums, lilies, meconopsis, shortias and many other plants. Different levels can be created, using peat blocks which themselves become part of the growing medium. Peat beds are often the only way to grow some of the most tricky rhododendrons and acid loving plants, but it is not just a planting site for the rare and difficult. A well-planted peat garden will provide year–round interest through a mixture of rhododendrons, *Ericaceae*, bulbs and perennials. Peat beds are ideal for the gardener short of space, as they allow such a huge quantity and variety of plants to be grown in a small area.

HARDY HYBRIDS

These are the large-flowered hybrids which form most people's conception of the typical rhododendron. Generally speaking, hardy hybrids can be grown in the open in a fairly exposed site, and they are popular as providers of shelter and screening, as well as for their ornamental role. They are mostly large plants, growing to 2 × 2 m (6½ × 6½ ft) or more in 10 years, and eventually growing far bigger. Having said this, as younger plants they do make fine specimens for a small garden, and if they get too big, and the means to move them can be found, rhododendrons can be dug up and replanted quite easily, even at considerable size and age. The hardy hybrid group contains many of the most spectacular rhododendrons in flower, but in general, the foliage of these plants is fairly uniform and uninteresting. They can of course be mixed with larger species to provide a contrast of foliage and flowers, but bear in mind that species generally require a more sheltered and favourable site while hardy hybrids are most useful for the less favourable areas of the garden. The main advantage of hardy hybrids is their reliability; hardy hybrids will generally cover themselves in flower year after year from a young age while, in contrast, many species take years to start flowering and do not flower well every year.

From 'Nobleanum' in early to late winter and 'Christmas Cheer' in early to mid spring to the peak of flowering in late spring and early summer, the hardy hybrids, if well chosen, will provide a dependable spectacular show. For impact from a distance, the hardy hybrids are undoubtedly the best bet, while the subtleties of dwarfs and species are often better appreciated close up. In gardens with a severe climate, with excess cold, wind, heat or sun, the hardy hybrids generally provide the most satisfactory rhododendrons. Many have been bred to provide cold hardiness in temperatures as low as −32°C (−25°F), or as high as 38°C (100°F), so there are few gardens where at least some hardy hybrid rhododendrons cannot be grown successfully. In warmer and sunnier climates, the later flowering hybrids will normally need some shade to allow the flowers to last more than a few days. For climates with really strong sun, there are some hardy hybrids with particularly sun-tolerant leaves. These include 'Fastuosum Flore Pleno', 'Gomer Waterer',

'President Roosevelt', most striking variegated rhododendron; the flowers are red and white.

'Jean Marie de Montague', 'Nova Zembla' and several others.

Associating other plants with hardy hybrids is comparatively easy. The hardy hybrids are more vigorous and less fastidious as to conditions, and so can put up with a certain amount of competition from other plants. In a large garden, sweeps of lawn bordered by beds of hardy hybrids, perhaps surrounded by naturalized bulbs such as daffodils and snowdrops, give an effective show. The general rule is that as long as the associated plants do not provide excessive shade or competition for moisture, any plant which likes similar soil conditions makes a suitable companion.

WOODLAND HYBRIDS

These are generally hybrids whose parentage contains more tender species than those used for the hardy hybrids. Often the hybrids are primary crosses between two species, so can be close to their parents in appearance and requirements. These hybrids generally need more shelter, and are less rugged than the hardy hybrids. Many hybrids with pure red, pastel, orange and yellow flowers such as 'Fabia', 'Lady Chamberlain' and 'Vanessa Pastel' fall into this category. In the following chapter, where recommended hybrids are listed, those rated H4 and H5 are considered to be 'hardy hybrids' while those rated H2 and H3 are 'woodland hybrids'. Woodland hybrids like similar conditions to the larger species described in the next section.

LARGER SPECIES

Most of the great rhododendron collections of the world gain much of their impact from larger-growing species. The extraordinary variety of foliage which sets off the huge range of flower shapes, sizes and colours has few equals. Although some larger species are hardy enough to withstand an exposed site, the majority of those most prized for their flowers and foliage require a certain amount of shelter. Many larger species flower rather early, so are rather vulnerable to having their flowers spoiled by frost some years, in all but the mildest areas. In addition, many species come into growth early and frosted growth, unlike frosted flowers, results in permanent damage, at best frost-distorted growth, at worst bark split, and even death. In the autumn some species are slow to harden off their growth, and therefore sites sheltered from early autumn frosts are desirable. Away from the mildest areas, by giving wind shelter, light shade, the protection of walls by planting on slopes, the local climate can usually be moderated to minimize weather damage.

Frosts are by no means the only problem. In winter, during cold but sunny or windy weather, the leaves rapidly lose moisture through evaporation, and if the plant cannot replenish its water due to frozen or dry ground, the cells in the leaves collapse, causing the plant to wilt. While this is not serious for short periods, it can be fatal if prolonged, and the provision of wind shelter and some shade is advisable to minimize this problem. Likewise new growth is vulnerable to sun and wind damage, and strong winds can blow off the leaves of the larger-leaved varieties at any time of year. As a general rule, the larger the leaf, the more wind-shelter and shade is required, although there are exceptions to this.

In more northern climates, most rhododendrons grow into the most shapely, free-flowering specimens with clear sky directly overhead. In hotter, sunnier climates however, larger species will usually require a degree of overhead shade to avoid sunburned leaves, to prevent the soil from warming up too much, and to allow flowers to last longer. Choose trees which provide filtered light, and which do not have the greediest roots. Small-leaved maples, flowering cherries, almonds, rowans, oaks, dogwoods, apples, birches and many other trees, especially conifers, are suitable. Sycamores, beech and other trees have very greedy roots and thick canopies, and very few plants can grow successfully underneath them.

The high walls, hedges, and surrounding buildings of town gardens often produce perfectly suitable conditions comparable to those of light woodland. Funnelling wind can be cut out by judicious tree or hedge planting, while walls provide some of the most favourable sites to grow tender species and hybrids. Straggly hybrids such as 'Fragrantissimum' can be trained onto a wall as an informal fan. Even some of the trickiest rhododendron species can thrive in such urban conditions. You certainly don't need acres of land for a woodland effect; a few trees and shrubs judiciously placed in the corner of a small garden can create a 'woodland' area for several medium-sized rhododendrons and some associated plants. An alternative strategy is to build a lath house which provides wind shelter and shade but which, unlike natural shelter from trees and shrubs, doesn't grow too big, or compete with your rhododendrons! Unfortunately of course, it doesn't look so nice either. Aim for 30–50% shade, depending on the wind and sun problems. The roof can be designed to provide more or less shade than the walls. In addition to providing shade and wind shelter, lath houses will usually give several degrees of frost protection.

□ A LARGE WOODLAND GARDEN

To plant a larger woodland garden there are basically two ways to start, depending on whether you already have a suitable wooded area or not. If you have some existing woodland, it will almost certainly need thinning. Make substantial clearings so that your rhododendrons do not have to compete directly with the trees; the latter would invariably win the battle for moisture. Shade from too many trees invariably causes the rhododendrons to grow upwards towards the light, producing sparse, ugly and unhealthy plants. It is much easier to clear sufficient woodland in one go before starting to plant, than to try to fell trees among planted rhododendrons. Retain your best shelter according to your commonest prevailing winds, and be careful not to remove trees which will leave others more vulnerable to storm damage. Mature trees tend to protect and support one another to some extent, so it is usually important to select trees to fell very carefully. Try to keep as much natural undergrowth as possible around the planting areas, as this forms an important part of the shelter; some extra planting may well be required at ground level to augment it. Old tree-stumps tend to harbour honey fungus (see p.104), and although stumps are very hard to remove, it is worth trying to get rid of small ones.

If you have to start a woodland garden from scratch, ideally the trees should be planted several years before the rhododendrons, but of course this is rarely practicable. Planting a mixture of broadleaved trees, fast growing conifers such as × *Cupressocyparis* 'Leylandii' and its relations, and evergreen shrubs such as hollies and laurels, will give some wind shelter in the least time. Artificial barriers are useful to protect the newly planted shelter belt, and to allow it to establish most quickly. As far as the rhododendrons are concerned, concentrate on smaller growing, hardier and more wind-tolerant varieties until good shelter is established.

Whichever type of woodland garden you have, vigorous hardy hybrids and hardier species can be successfully used to shelter more tender varieties. 'Cunningham's White', 'Gomer Waterer', 'Cynthia', 'Fastuosum Flore Pleno' *R. rubiginosum* and *R. decorum* are all suitable as shelter, windbreaks or infor-

mal hedges. Too much reliance on deciduous trees and shrubs in the shelter belt can obviously result in times of year when the protection is not adequate; a really dense mixture of evergreen and deciduous plants is ideal. In more inland gardens, underplant with hardy conifers, laurels, hollies, quickthorn and other plants. There is no need to regard a shelter belt as unornamental; incorporating colourful plants such as the taller growing berberis, variegated hollies, cotoneaster, and others with coloured foliage and berries can help to provide year-round interest. In milder coastal gardens, high winds and salt spray are often a problem. Shelter can be provided by sycamore, spruce and pines, underplanted with *Escallonia*, *Griselinia* and *Olearia* and other plants. In the u.k. some people use the invasive 'wild' *R. ponticum* as shelter. This is fine in areas of low rainfall, but in southern and western gardens in Britain where *R. ponticum* is a pest, it will soon get out of control, and it is virtually impossible to eradicate.

Some woodland rhododendron species, such as those in the Triflora subsection (*R. augustinii*, *R. yunnanense* and others; see p.63), can be planted in groups which will eventually join up. Many other species, especially those with the largest leaves, are best planted with plenty of room to grow unhindered by surrounding plants, where they can form fairly symmetrical specimens clothed to the ground. Most people tend to plant fairly close together so that the plants make an impact after the minimum amount of time. If you do this, it is

A red form of R. arboreum. *Most red forms are only suitable for milder areas.*

R. barbatum, *one of the finest red-flowered species which has the additional bonus of beautiful peeling bark.*

important to thin out or move plants to prevent overcrowding. Large-leaved species, such as *R. calophytum*, *R. macabeanum*, *R. falconeri* and *R. rex*, have magnificent foliage, and can grow into trees of 6 × 6m (20 × 20ft), and even more in the most favourable gardens, so ultimately they need plenty of room, and should be planted with a view to allowing them to become striking individual specimens. Rhododendrons and azaleas do not mind being moved even at a very large size. The problem here is more a lack of human strength to dig them up!

Within even a small garden, microclimates exist which produce variations in climatic severity and which therefore dictate appropriate sites for different species. Frost flows downhill, causing colder temperatures in hollows than on mounds. Frost can be trapped in low-lying, very sheltered areas (frost pockets), so although these areas may be favourable from the point of view of wind shelter, they will not be suitable for tender or early-flowering rhododendron varieties. Even within a small area there can be up to 3°C (6°F) of variation in temperature during frost, and this can often be enough to make the difference between damage and escaping unscathed. Also, early morning sun can ruin flower buds by fast alternate freezing and thawing. If you can identify your frost pockets, use them for hardier and later-flowering and late-growing varieties, keeping the earlier-flowering and more tender ones for the warmer sites. If you find that one variety is constantly damaged in one

site, don't hesitate to move it; that often makes all the difference, even if the move is only a matter of metres (yards).

DECIDUOUS AZALEAS

Deciduous azaleas are perhaps the brightest-coloured members of the rhododendron genus. A wide range of flower colours is available; white, pink, yellow, orange, red and combinations of these. Some have fine autumn colours and many of the paler coloured ones have a strong scent. They are easy to grow, in sun or light woodland, and most are tolerant of wind.

The one disadvantage of deciduous azaleas is the fact that they are deciduous, and so do not contribute the year-round greenery of the other groups. For this reason they are usually used as background planting, in bold groups if space permits. There is no reason not to mix them with rhododendron species or hybrids, although my own preference is not to mix up the brightest-flowered azalea hybrids with rhododendrons. Having said that, there are fine colour contrasts to be found between purple rhododendron hybrids such as 'Purple Splendour', and the yellow and orange azaleas.

In addition to the hybrids, several azalea species are available. Some of them, notably *R. schlippenbachii* and *R. albrechtii*, tend to grow early and need woodland protection outside favourable areas. *R. occidentale* also occasionally comes into growth early, but it can generally take full exposure. Species from south-eastern U.S.A., for instance

R. calendulaceum, are particularly sun- and heat-tolerant.

For mass effect in flower, few shrubs can equal the display of groups of deciduous azalea hybrids. These can usually be bought most cheaply as un-named seedlings by colour. Unlike rhododendron hybrids from seed, deciduous azalea strains provide a high percentage of fine seedlings, certainly good enough for massed display. Named hybrids are preferable if you only have room for a few plants.

JAPANESE OR EVERGREEN AZALEAS

These are evergreen or semi-evergreen, low-growing or medium-sized plants, with flowers ranging from purple, through red, and many shades of pink to white. So far no one has managed to breed a yellow one. In general, these azaleas like hotter, drier conditions, and are more heat-tolerant than dwarf rhododendrons, allowing them to be grown very successfully in places such as Virginia and Georgia, U.S.A., where most rhododendrons suffer heat damage. They are also very successful in most other rhododendron growing areas, although in cooler climates such as Scotland, north-west Germany, and eastern Canada, only a small percentage of the hundreds of hybrids available do really well. These are noted in Chapter 3. In such cooler climates these azaleas should be grown in full sun to allow the new wood to ripen sufficiently to withstand the following winter. In hotter or sunnier climates, light shade is ideal,

allowing the bright flower colours to last without bleaching. Due to their slightly different cultural requirements, and also due to the very 'hot' colours of many of them, I would recommend growing Japanese azaleas in groups rather than mixed up with dwarf rhododendrons. Several gardens such as Windsor Great Park, near London, have massed displays of these azaleas, and even in a very small garden an effective blaze of contrasting colours can be made with a clump of three or more. Unlike deciduous azaleas, they should not be bought as unnamed seedlings unless you can see them in flower beforehand. Evergreen azaleas make good container plants as they enjoy drier and hotter conditions than rhododendrons, and they are popular plants for bonsai.

PLANTING IN TUBS AND CONTAINERS

Although some people are very successful at growing rhododendrons in containers outdoors, as a general rule rhododendrons and azaleas are not the most satisfactory plants for this purpose. Invariably the container is allowed to dry out, and the rhododendron takes on a yellow, starved appearance. The container often heats up and is vulnerable to freezing in the winter, both of which are detrimental to healthy rhododendrons. Having said this, certain easy hardy hybrids such as 'Fastuosum Flore Pleno' and 'Cunningham's White', and hardy evergreen azaleas, can often be grown healthily in containers. In areas of very alkaline soil, it may be the

R. cinnabarinum, *a variable species seen in many different colours.*

only way to grow rhododendrons at all. In such areas, be careful not to water the container with alkaline water; rainwater can be collected to avoid this problem. Some very dwarf species and hybrids are suitable for trough gardens, but you will need to use companion plants which like acid soil and similarly moist soil conditions.

Tender species and hybrids, especially those of the Maddenia and Edgeworthia subsections make fine container plants, allowing them to be grown in colder areas. These can be brought into the house in flower, plunged outdoors for the summer and kept in a greenhouse or conservatory in winter (see the next section). For all container planting, the compost must be well drained but also able to retain enough moisture. A mixture of some or all of peat, bark or sand, leafmould and conifer needles is ideal.

RHODODENDRONS INDOORS

Everyone is familiar with the azaleas grown as houseplants. Many people have trouble looking after them, the principal reason being that usually the pot that they are bought in is too small, and is impossible to keep adequately watered. Repot these azaleas into a larger container in peaty compost with fertilizer (see Chapter 4) and do not allow them to dry out. They can be plunged outdoors during frost-free weather and brought in again to flower during the winter or spring.

The other group of rhododendrons most commonly grown as houseplants are the scented pinks and whites of the Maddenia and Edgeworthia species. Many of these are too tender to grow outside except in the most favourable climates, and need the protection of a cold greenhouse. The hot dry atmosphere of most centrally-heated homes is not really suitable for these rhododendrons; they are most successful in a greenhouse or conservatory, only being brought into the house when in flower. If you don't have a greenhouse, a well-lit, cool room in the house may be successful. Indoor rhododendrons can be put outside during the summer, plunged into the ground to keep the pot cool if possible. If they are left in a greenhouse in summer, ensure that the area is well-ventilated and keep the air moist by damping down the floor.

Many tender species and hybrids can be grown in an unheated greenhouse or conservatory, planted in the soil, or with the pots plunged in soil or cinders. In a heated greenhouse, set the temperature at the minimum to keep the frost out; too much heat causes the flower buds to drop off. During mild winter weather, the greenhouse or conservatory should be well-ventilated to avoid problems such as grey mould (botrytis).

Many of the scented rhododendrons are very straggly, even if well-pruned. They can be successfully grown and trained against a wall, and some such as 'Fragrantissimum' can be tied around stakes pushed into the pot. Plant indoor rhododendrons in a well-drained ericaceous compost, or make up your own from acid loam, peat and leafmould or

R. macabeanum, *one of the stunning large-leaved species. This form is from Trewithen Gardens in Cornwall.*

conifer needles. For the adventurous, tropical Vireya species and hybrids can be grown, either in containers or planted in a bed. Although Vireyas are generally quite free flowering, they are notoriously straggly and hard to keep healthy. They need a compost with a particularly high proportion of decomposing organic matter and like very good drainage.

CHAPTER THREE

CHOOSING THE BEST

The following chapter gives a selection of 60 rhododendron species, 130 hybrids and a selection of deciduous and evergreen azaleas. This is only a fraction of what is available; there are hundreds of other rhododendrons and azalea species and hybrids, not listed here, which are also well worth growing. The selection given represents a broad sweep of what is available, from the tallest to the smallest, the hardiest to the most tender, from the best scent to the best foliage. Start with some of the easier-to-please species and hybrids, and then become more adventurous.

BUYING RHODODENDRONS

Your local garden centre will probably have a range of the commonest hybrids and azaleas, but you will be lucky to find more than a small selection. On the whole, larger species do not grow well in containers and they are generally only available from specialist nurseries. Such nurseries usually offer a wide selection of species and hybrids, including many not listed in this book. Most provide a descriptive catalogue, many have a mail order service and some are prepared to export. Prices and quality vary enormously, so shop around. Rhododendrons are hard to identify and are often wrongly named by the uninitiated, so if you care about receiving authentically named species and hybrids, only buy them from reputable sources. Rhododendrons are produced commercially by a number of different methods, each one having its own advantages and disadvantages from the point of view of the buyer.

Most of the common varieties are produced from cuttings, small shoots rooted in compost. A plant grown from a cutting is asexually or vegetatively reproduced, so it is genetically identical to its parent. Named or award clones of species, and all named hybrids must be produced asexually. An unhybridized seedling of *R. yakushimanum* 'Koichiro Wada' F.C.C. is still the species *yakushimanum*, but is no longer the F.C.C. clone. It will be different from its parent, and may be inferior or even superior. A seedling of the hybrid 'Elizabeth' is NOT 'Elizabeth', and will almost certainly be inferior. Life would be easy if all rhododendrons could be produced from cuttings, but unfortunately many species and some hybrids are very hard or impossible to root, so other methods are used. Other vegetative methods used include layering, grafting and micropropagation.

Layers are shoots which are bent down so that they root into the soil (see p.114). The only problem with layers is that they tend to have a bend at the base of the plant where it was anchored to the soil. Judicious pruning can usually produce a good plant.

Grafting involves making a union between a hard-to-root shoot and a rootstock. This is often the only method to produce selected clones of species and hard-to-root hybrids. The main problem with grafts is that the rootstock often throws out suckers, which can swamp the plant grafted on top if they are not removed (suckers should be broken off, not cut). *R. ponticum* has traditionally been used as a rootstock, but it is too vigorous, regularly throwing suckers, and plants grafted on to *R. ponticum* are not recommended. If you buy grafted plants, enquire what rootstock was used. If you can't get an answer, assume it was *R. ponticum* and don't buy. Plants grafted on 'Cunningham's White' and other rootstocks impart a degree of alkalinity tolerance and several other benefits. Grafted plants are the norm in parts of Europe for all larger hybrids, as they grow better there than plants on their own roots.

Micropropagation is a new technique

(Above) R. pachysanthum, *a fine, newly-discovered, medium-sized species with attractive flowers and foliage.*

(Below) R. williamsianum, *a fine dwarf species with pink bell-shaped flowers and coppery new growth.*

which involves cloning tiny plantlets in test-tubes, using hormones. They make perfectly good plants, often bushier than those from cuttings. There have been a few teething problems with this method, but if a micropropagated plant looks vigorous and healthy, it should grow very well.

Growing from seed involves sexual reproduction, so the offspring are not genetically identical to the parents. Named hybrids CANNOT be reproduced by seed. Although hybrids are all raised from seed in the first place, the resulting seedlings are all unique plants, some good, some bad, some average, and they have to be grown on to flowering size, tested, selected and named, and the named selections then have to be propagated from cuttings or other vegetative means.

Species CAN be grown from seed, either collected in the wild, or pollinated in gardens. The problem with the latter is that in gardens, rhododendrons are very readily crossed by insects, and they must be deliberately hand-pollinated to avoid contaminated hybrid seed. Species grown from open-pollinated seed should be avoided, as the bees probably will have visited every other rhododendron in the vicinity, and the resulting seedlings will almost certainly be hybrids. A few nurseries, including our own, regularly hand-pollinate seed to raise species. Each seedling will be unique, and different from the parents, but it will be an authentic example of the species. When hand-pollinating, it is important to use only the best forms of species as parents

to ensure the best offspring. The resultant seedlings will probably produce some plants of equal or better quality than the parents. The advantage of seedlings is that they are cheaper to produce than grafts, they usually produce more compact plants, and they do not have the risk of understock suckering. The disadvantage is the variation in quality which results.

Growing plants from wild seed is another alternative. Some nurseries grow species from seed collected in the Himalayas and elsewhere. Wild seed is even more variable than garden hand-pollinated seed, but collectors usually select seed from plants from the highest altitude (for hardiness), with the largest flowers, best foliage and other attractive or distinct characteristics. Most collectors use numbers to designate each collection of seed. *R. wardii* L. & S. 5679 refers to the collectors Ludlow and Sherriff. It is possible to look up this number and find out the whole history of the original seed. The number refers to an expedition to Tibet in 1938; the seed was collected at a place called Molo, at 3670m (11 000ft). These and other details are given in Ludlow and Sherriff's field notes. Many people find these collector's numbers a nuisance, but they greatly increase the value and interest of a collection, and are well worth recording on the plant's label, and in separate records. If you find that a particularly fine plant results from wild (or hand-pollinated) seed, it may well be worth naming, may deserve an award, and will probably be sought after by other collectors. If you have space,

EXPLANATION OF DESCRIPTIONS.

g. – grex. **A Link of its own**
Signifies that several different plants exist under one name. Usually the best clones have an award, e.g. A.M., or a clonal name e.g. 'Venus' or both e.g. 'Naomi Exbury A.M.'

Hardiness rating
This is the lowest temperature which the plant can withstand without suffering severe damage or death. Some damage may occur at higher temperatures. Very dependent on local conditions e.g. wind shelter, and on timing of cold weather.

H5 – 23°C (– 10°F)
H4 – 18°C (0°F)
H3 – 15°C (5°F)
H2 – 12°C (10°F)
H1 – 10/ – 8°C (14/18°F)

Approximate height in 10 years. This depends on climate, moisture, shade, etc.

Dwarf	under 45 cm (1½ ft)
Semi-dwarf	45 – 80 cm (1½ – 3 ft)
Low	80 – 135 cm (3 – 4½ ft)
Medium	135 – 180 cm (4½ – 6 ft)
Tall	180 cm + (6 ft +)

'Lady Chamberlain' g.

Medium-Tall   H3–4   M

One of the many hybrids raised from the species *cinnabarinum*, which passes on its clusters of pendulous waxy flowers to its offspring. 'Lady Chamberlain' has salmon-orange or orange-pink flowers (depending on the clone). Small leaves on an airy, upright bush. Needs wind shelter, and not for coldest gardens. F.C.C. 1967. In common with *R. cinnabarinum* itself, its hybrids are very prone to powdery mildew which can defoliate or even kill plants (p. 105). Other similar hybrids include 'Lady Rosebery' F.C.C. Pink flowers; 'Alison Johnstone' A.M. pale peachy-apricot flowers; 'Trewithen Orange' F.C.C. soft orange flowers; 'Cinnkeys' A.M., orange and red tubular flowers.

Description of flower

Description of foliage/habit

Special requirements/problems

Other similar species/hybrids

Flowering time. Dates given below are for U.K. and Australia/New Zealand. In colder climates, the season is compressed, beginning in April. Exact flowering times vary from year to year.

Time	U.K.	AUST/NZ
VE very early	Dec – Feb	Jul
E Early	Mar	Aug
EM fairly early	April	Sept
M early mid	Early May	Early Oct
ML late mid	Late May	Late Oct
L late	June	Nov
VL very late	July – Aug	Dec

Awards given for good species selections and hybrids. Not all the best plants have awards, and not all awards are for good plants. Awards with 'T' were given after trials at Wisley Garden, Surrey, U.K.

F.C.C. (T.) First class certificate — highest award (U.K.)
A.M. (T.) Award of merit — second highest award (U.K.)
H.C. (T.) Highly commended (U.K.)
S.P.A. Superior plant award — highest award (U.S.A.)
A.E. Award of excellence — second highest award (U.S.A.)

wild seedlings are great fun to grow. Occasional disappointments are more than compensated for by the fine new forms which result. If you plant a clump of several plants from the same number, the poorer ones can be removed as flowering starts, allowing room for the best plants to mature.

All the propagation methods outlined above have their own advantages and shortcomings, and most nurseries use a combination of them to produce what they offer. The best nurseries indicate in their catalogue which method has been used, as this is obviously important when making your selection.

Species

R. arboreum

Medium/Tall   H2–4   E–ML

A very widespread and variable species which forms spectacular forests in Nepal and elsewhere, covering hillsides with flower. Flowers red, pink or white, sometimes bicoloured, in dense, conical trusses. The red forms are generally the most tender, only suitable for favourable gardens. Many pink and white forms are fairly hardy. Fine foliage, leaves have white, fawn or brown indumentum below. Generally

Rhododendrons and azaleas have a wide variety of flower and truss shapes. The line drawings on the following pages show five of the most common truss shapes described in the text of Chapter 3. Here is a conical/tall truss typical of some rhododendron species and many larger hybrids.

needs wind shelter, ideal in a woodland garden. Tree forms can reach up to 12 m (40 ft) in height, but some forms are lower and more bushy.

R. augustinii

Medium   H3–4   EM–M

One of the best blue rhododendron species. Flowers vary from pale lavender to deep violet-blue, in three-flower trusses. Unfortunately the deepest coloured forms are usually the most tender. Best planted in groups or with other similar species such as *R. yunnanense*. Small leaves on an airy upright bush. Parent of many smaller hybrids. See 'Blue Diamond', p.63.

R. auriculatum

Tall   H4–(5)   VL

The latest to flower of all species, well into late summer in the U.K. Loose trusses of scented, white or pale pink flowers, usually blotched green in the centre. Needs some shade to allow flowers to last, and best with some wind shelter. Grows very late in the season, although this makes it vulnerable to early frosts in colder gardens. See also 'Polar Bear'.

An example of a rounded truss, typical of many rhododendron species and larger and medium-sized hybrids.

R. barbatum

Medium/Tall   H3–4   VE–EM

An early flowered species which has everything – flowers, foliage and bark. The best forms have fine bright scarlet flowers in full, conical trusses. Stiff pointed leaves usually have bristles on the leaf stalks (hence the name). One of its best features is its smooth peeling bark which becomes an impressive feature on an older plant. Best in a sheltered site to avoid having the flowers frosted. Some clones are rather prone to powdery mildew. **R. strigillosum** has looser trusses of bright red flowers, opening equally early. Narrow leaves usually curve down at the edges.

R. bureavii

Low/Medium   H4–5   EM–M

One of the finest foliage plants in any genus, its deep green leaves and stems are covered with rufous brown indumentum. Flowers in loose trusses are pink or white, with red speckles. Hardy, but needs wind shelter to keep its foliage in best condition. Slow to start flowering, but well worth growing for its foliage alone.

R. calophytum

Tall   H5   VE–EM

The hardiest of the species with long leaves, which are up to 38 cm (15 in) in length. Although hardy, its leaves need

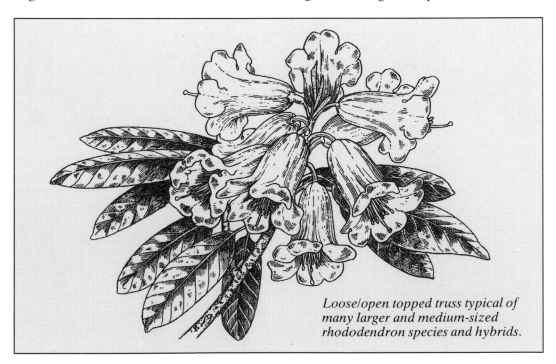

Loose/open topped truss typical of many larger and medium-sized rhododendron species and hybrids.

wind shelter, and its early flowers need a favourable site. Large loose to rounded trusses of white or pink flowers with a blotch or spotting of crimson in the centre of each. Leaves have no indumentum. Grows into a large, umbrella-shaped bush or tree.

R. calostrotum

Dwarf   H4–5   M

A very fine dwarf species with large, flat-faced flowers which are purple in most forms. One of the best of these is *R. calostrotum* 'Rock' which has large deep purple flowers and bluish foliage. It is taller growing than the excellent *R. calostrotum* 'Gigha' F.C.C. 1971, which has rose-crimson flowers on a

very dwarf bush with greyish foliage. This is one of the finest of all dwarfs. *R. keleticum*, closely-related, with flat-faced purple flowers, later than the above. The lowest-growing forms are from the Radicans group, probably the most dwarf of all rhododendrons.

R. campanulatum

Medium/Tall   H4–5   E–M

Compact to loose trusses of purple, mauve, magenta, lavender-pink or white flowers. Glossy leaves are up to 15 cm (6 in) in length, and have indumentum below. A variable species, the best forms are those with the largest leaves, or the nearest to blue or white flowers. Some forms are rather tender.

Lax truss typical of some medium-sized and low-growing rhododendron species and hybrids.

R. c. ssp. ***aeruginosum*** has a lower, more compact habit, and is mainly grown for its glaucous bluish-grey foliage found on the best forms. Forms a large bush or small tree.

R. campylocarpum

Low/Medium   H3–4   EM–M

One of the easiest to grow of the yellow-flowered species. Bell-shaped flowers in loose trusses are pale to light yellow, sometimes with a small red blotch. Avoid too much shade to obtain a free flowering, compact plant.
R. callimorphum is very similar, but with pink flowers; it's also usually less hardy.

R. campylogynum

Dwarf/Semi-dwarf   H3–4   EM–M

A varied but very distinct dwarf species with thimble-shaped flowers on stalks, held above the foliage. Flowers can be purple, claret, red, pink or white. Different forms vary in height from 8 cm (3 in) to 1 m (3¼ ft), the majority being neat, compact and low growing. It is well worth growing a selection of these. Not good in hot or dry sites.

R. cinnabarinum

Medium   H3–4   EM–L

Certainly one of the most distinctive

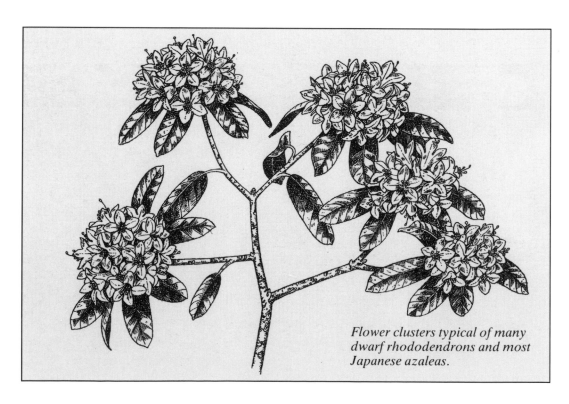

Flower clusters typical of many dwarf rhododendrons and most Japanese azaleas.

'*Anna Baldsiefen*', *a very free flowering, American, dwarf hybrid.*

rhododendron species. Clusters of waxy, tubular flowers in hanging clusters. Small leaves on a generally open, airy bush of slender habit. Many coloured forms exist, red, purple, pink, yellow, orange and red and orange. Ssp. *xanthocodon* has yellow flowers, while the Concatenans Gp. has orange ones. Leaves need shelter from cold winds. Unfortunately these species and their hybrids such as 'Lady Chamberlain' are very susceptible to powdery mildew (see p.105).

R. dauricum

Semi-dwarf/Medium   H5   VE–EM

One of the hardiest of all species, some forms can survive in temperatures as low as −32°C (−25°F). Flowers usually pale to rosy purple, some forms have pinker or white flowers. Most forms are deciduous or semi-deciduous, usually flowering on bare stems. Leaves usually turn bronzy or red in the autumn. The flowers of most forms will tolerate some frost, so worth growing even in severe gardens. Two of the best forms are 'Midwinter', F.C.C. purple; usually the earliest rhododendrons to flower, often before Christmas in the U.K., and 'Hokkaido', large white flowers later in the season. *R. mucronulatum* is very similar, but has pink, rosy purple, occasionally white flowers and is usually slightly later flowering.

R. decorum

Medium/Tall   H3–4   M–L

One of the best scented rhododendrons for general planting. Large trusses of pale pink or white flowers. A vigorous, upright grower which succeeds in drier sites and more alkaline soils than most rhododendrons. Variable in hardiness, so worth seeking the toughest forms. Easy to please, and highly recommended.

R. dichroanthum

Low   H4   M–L

One of the few orange-flowered species. Waxy flowers in lax trusses of various shades of orange, red, pink and yellow, often a combination of these colours. The orange forms are usually the most striking. A compact grower with dense foliage; leaves indumented below. Needs good drainage. Many forms are rather shy-flowering.

R. falconeri

Tall   H3–(4)   EM–L

One of the finest large-leaved species. Large, open-topped trusses of long-lasting, creamy white to pale yellow flowers, deeply blotched purple in the centre. Leaves up to 30cm (12in) long have a rusty indumentum below. Needs wind shelter or a woodland site *R.f.* ssp. *eximium* is slightly lower-growing with pink to cream flowers and very fine indumentum on both surfaces of the leaves.

R. fastigiatum

Dwarf   H5   EM–M

One of the easiest of all species to grow.

'Baden Baden', one of the German hardy, low-growing, red hybrids. 'Elisabeth Hobbie' and 'Scarlet Wonder' are very similar.

Clusters of light to deep purple-blue flowers on a neat, compact bush with small leaves which are usually greyish-blue. Very free flowering, hardy and tolerant of full exposure. *R. impeditum*, very similar but usually has greenish rather than blue leaves. Often confused with *R. fastigiatum* in commerce. *R. russatum*, a related species with deeper coloured flowers, in shades of purple. The best forms are of rich, deep colours. Varied in habit from compact to straggly. Makes a fine contrast planted with yellow-flowered dwarfs.

R. ferrugineum

Dwarf/Semi–dwarf   H5   L–VL

The well-known Alpenrose from the Alps and Pyrenees mountains. Clusters of small pale to deep pink flowers. Useful for its late flowering. A compact, spreading grower which is hardy and easy to please. *R. hirsutum*, similar, but has hairy leaves, paler flowers and is tolerant of fairly alkaline soils.

R. forrestii

Dwarf   H4   E–M

Waxy, pure crimson and scarlet flowers in lax trusses on a low, dense plant with small, rounded leaves. A difficult plant to please, as it dislikes hot sun, heat and dry conditions. A well-drained, north-facing bank is ideal. Choose only the most free-flowering forms. Forms under the name *R. forrestii* Repens Gp. are the lowest growing, with a creeping habit. Fairly hardy, but sometimes produces early growth.

R. fortunei

Medium/Tall   H5   M–L

The hardiest of the scented species. Open-topped trusses of fragrant white or pale lilac flowers. A vigorous grower with shiny leaves. Robust and easy to please.

R. griersonianum

Low/Medium   H2/3   L–VL

This species has been much used in hybridizing to pass on its freedom of flowering and pure red colour. Bright geranium-scarlet flowers in loose trusses, on a rangy bush best grown with plenty of overhead light. Tends to grow late in the season, so can be vulnerable to frosts. Most successful in warmer coastal regions. Its hybrids such as 'Vulcan' and 'Elizabeth' are better for colder gardens.

R. haematodes

Semi-dwarf/Low   H4   M–ML

A popular, low-growing species with fleshy, scarlet or crimson flowers in lax to loose trusses. A neat, compact shrub, densely clad with dark leaves, indumented below. Needs good drainage.

R. hodgsonii

Medium/Tall   H4   EM–M

Found wild in Nepal and Bhutan, this is one of the hardiest of the large-leaved species. Very variable flowers; shades of pink, red or purple, usually fading, in large, compact trusses. Long leaves have buff or grey indumentum beneath. Needs wind shelter.

R. insigne

Low/Medium   H5   M–L

A fine, hardy species with loose to rounded trusses of pink flowers. Medium-sized, pointed, thick, leathery leaves have an unusual indumentum below which has a metallic sheen. A tidy compact grower if planted in an open site. Especially useful for its late flowering and hardiness. *R. argyrophyllum* is a related species with white to silvery indumentum on the lower leaf surface. Flowers white or pink.

R. irroratum

Low/Medium   H3–4   E–M

A variable species which is only really worth growing in its better forms. Freely-produced, loose trusses of white or pink flowers, sometimes deeply spotted red or purple. Leaves undistinguished. A popular clone is 'Polka Dot' A.M. which has pink flowers, heavily spotted purple.

R. lacteum

Low/Medium   H4   EM–M

A species for the enthusiast. Pale to medium yellow flowers in full, rounded trusses, sometimes blotched crimson. Rounded leaves have a thin indumentum below. Rather hard to please, preferring some shade, good

drainage, and very acid soil. Grafted plants are sometimes more successful than those on their own roots.

R. lindleyi

Low/Medium   H2–3   EM–M

One of the most spectacular of the tender, scented species. Flowers not unlike lily trumpets, in lax to loose trusses, are white, usually with some yellow and pink, and are strongly scented. A straggly grower, best against a wall or planted in a group where a tangled thicket can form. There are many other similar species, all with scented white, pink tinged flowers. Two of the best are *R. edgeworthii*, a more compact grower with rough grooved leaves, and *R. formosum*, more upright with small leaves. These species are only suitable for the greenhouse and conservatory in coldest gardens, but in their hardier forms they can be successfully grown outdoors in a favourable site such as a partly shaded wall, even in moderately severe climates.

R. macabeanum

Tall   H3–4   E–M

A spectacular species with very large, loose trusses of yellow flowers, blotched purple. Large leaves, up to 30 cm (12 in) long, have a white or fawn indumentum below. Its spectacular new growth is an added bonus. Needs wind shelter. A very large grower in favourable conditions. *R. sinogrande* has similar flowers, is equally large, but is less hardy. It has the largest leaves of any rhododendron, up to 90cm (3ft) and is well worth growing in a sheltered garden with plenty of room.

R. maddenii

Medium/Tall   H2–3   M–VL

A very variable species, formerly under many different names. White to creamy-pink, sweetly-scented flowers, sometimes marked deeper. Tender, generally only suitable for milder and coastal gardens. A large, sprawling plant, generally too large for pot cultivation. The hardiest forms are found under *R.m.* ssp. *crassum*.

R. niveum

Medium   H3–4   EM–M

Rounded trusses of smokey-blue or purple flowers (avoid the pinker or mauve forms). Not everyone's colour. Medium-sized leaves with near white indumentum below on a neat, compact bush. Needs wind shelter.

R. orbiculare

Low/Medium   H4   EM–M

A distinct species with medium-sized, smooth, pale green, virtually round leaves. Loose trusses of bell-shaped, bright pink flowers. Should be grown in

'Carita', an Exbury hybrid available in several colour forms.

plenty of light to ensure a compact, domed specimen.

R. oreodoxa

Medium   H4–5   E–EM

An easy and versatile, early-flowered species. White to pink and lilac flowers in loose trusses on a vigorous bush which forms a small tree. Opening buds and flowers will stand a few degrees of frost, managing to put on a show most years. Oval, smooth, pale green leaves curl up in hot sun or frost. **R. o. fargesii** is useful for its tolerance of heavy and clay soils. **R. vernicosum** is a similar species with slightly later flowers in a larger truss. Not quite as tough as *R. oreodoxa*. Flowers in shades of pink and lavender-pink.

R. pachysanthum

Low/Medium   H4   EM

A very fine, recently-introduced species. Pale pink to white flowers, spotted red or green, in rounded trusses. A compact bush with attractive pointed leaves which have silvery to fawn indumentum above, and brown indumentum below. May be hardier than rated, but its rather early flowers can be frosted. One of the best medium-sized species for foliage.

R. ponticum

Medium   H4   ML–L

The well-known or infamous 'wild' species. Rounded to conical trusses of lilac/purplish pink flowers. A vigorous, spreading bush which is very invasive, as it readily naturally layers and seeds itself. A useful plant for screening and shelter in areas of low rainfall. Uncontrollable in warmer, wetter areas of southern and western Britain, and should not be planted there, as it is a serious environmental pest.

R. pseudochrysanthum

Dwarf/Medium   H4–5   EM–M

A distinctive species from Taiwan. A compact bush with densely-packed, pointed leaves. Loose trusses of white or pale pink flowers, usually with red spotting. Different forms vary in height from under 15 cm (6 in) to over 3 m (10 ft). Best in light shade and with little fertilizer, to avoid browning of leaf tips.

R. racemosum

Semi-dwarf/Medium   H3–4(5)   E–M

A distinctive species, variable in size and hardiness. Masses of pink flowers in racemes (clusters up the stems). Small leaves on pinkish or reddish stems. Some forms are very rangy and benefit from pruning, or cutting in flower for the house. Dwarf and compact forms also exist. Very free flowering.

R. rex

Tall   H4   EM/M

Probably the most versatile and hardy of the large-leaved, indumented species. Large, full, rounded trusses of white to pink with crimson spotting. Deep green leaves, up to 45 cm (18 in), with buff indumentum below. Needs plenty of room to grow into a fine specimen. *R. r.* ssp. *fictolacteum* is very similar but with smaller leaves, deeper-coloured indumentum, and usually more spotting in the flower. Both take several years to flower.

R. roxieanum Oreonastes Gp

Semi–dwarf/Low   H5   EM–M

One of a group of rhododendrons called the Taliensia which are connoisseurs' favourites due to their interesting foliage. Long, narrow, pointed leaves with indumentum below, on a neat, compact plant, giving a spiky effect, unlike any other species. Full rounded trusses of white to pink flowers, spotted red. Takes some years to start flowering but worth growing for its foliage alone.

R. rubiginosum

Medium/Tall   H4   E–EM

A very vigorous, small-leaved species which makes a fine windbreak or informal hedge. Plentiful small flowers of lavender, mauve or rose are especially effective en masse. Choose hardier forms for more severe cold gardens. Good in drier and near-neutral soils.

R. souliei

Low/Medium   H4–5   M–ML

Open, saucer-shaped, pink or white flowers in loose trusses on a fairly compact bush with smooth rounded leaves. Needs very good drainage, and

wind protection for its early growth, but otherwise fairly hardy. An enthusiast's species.

R. thomsonii

Tall   H4   E–M

A fine larger species with showy, waxy, deep blood-red flowers in loose trusses. Rounded leaves are often bluish in the best forms. Forms a tree, showing off its fine, smooth, peeling bark. Unfortunately this species is one of the most susceptible to powdery mildew.

R. trichostomum

Semi-dwarf   H(3)–4   M–ML

One of a group of distinctive and attractive species with rounded clusters of small flowers which resemble those of daphnes. *R. trichostomum* has pink or white flowers. Some forms are tender, and should be avoided. One of the best clones is 'Collingwood Ingram' F.C.C. with rose flowers. Amongst the other related species are *R. primuliflorum* which is similar to the above, but flowering earlier in the season, and *R. sargentianum* which is more dwarf, with yellow or cream flowers. The above species all resent fertilizer, and soil which is too acid.

R. tsariense

Semi-dwarf/Low   H4   E–EM

A very fine smaller species with excellent foliage. The small, dark leaves have a fawn or rusty indumentum below, and a whitish one above on the

'Christmas Cheer', a very easily grown, hardy hybrid which flowers in early spring.

new growth. Pink and white flowers with red spotting. Rather early into flower and growth, so avoid frost pockets.

R. wardii

Low/Medium   H4/5   M–L

The most popular larger yellow species. Loose trusses of pale to deep yellow flowers, sometimes blotched red. Of medium habit, compact in an open site, with smooth oval leaves. Forms collected by Ludlow and Sherriff are amongst the best available; these need perfect drainage. Almost all larger-flowered yellow hybrids have some *wardii* in their parentage.

R. williamsianum

Semi-dwarf/Low   H4   EM–M

Easily recognized by its small, nearly round, smooth leaves which are bronzy when they first unfurl. Loose trusses of pink flowers. Best in an open site to obtain a striking, dense, compact plant. Early into growth, so not for frost pockets. A parent of many hybrids (see under 'Linda' and 'Moonstone' in the hybrid section).

R. yakushimanum

Semi-dwarf/Low   H5   M–ML

One of the most popular of all species, and many people's choice as the ultimate rhododendron. Pink buds open to full, rounded trusses of white flowers. Deep green leaves, curled downwards at the edges, with indumentum below, on a dense, slow-growing, compact bush. Free flowering and tough. One of the best forms is 'Koichiro Wada' F.C.C. The species is renowned for its hardiness, compactness and good foliage. Other good hybrids are 'Golden Torch', 'Dopey' and 'Bashful'.

□ **SOME OF THE BEST SPECIES BY COLOUR**

RED – *R. barbatum, R. forrestii, R. griersonianum, R. thomsonii*
WHITE – *R. decorum, R. lindleyi, R. rigidum, R. yakushimanum*
PINK – *R. oreodoxa, R. racemosum, R. souliei* pink forms, *R. williamsianum*
YELLOW – *R. campylocarpum, R. cinnabarinum* ssp. *xanthocodon, R. macabeanum, R. sinogrande, R. wardii*
PURPLE/BLUE – *R. augustinii, R. fastigiatum, R. keleticum, R. niveum, R. russatum*

□ **EASY SPECIES FOR THE SMALL GARDEN**

R. fastigiatum, R. ferrugineum, R. impeditum, R. keleticum, R. williamsianum, R. yakushimanum

□ **EASY SPECIES FOR THE LARGER GARDEN**

R. arboreum, R. bureavii, R. decorum, R. oreodoxa, R. rex ssp. *fictolacteum, R. rubiginosum, R. wardii, R. yunnanense*

R. yunnanense

Medium/Tall   H3–4   M–ML

One of a group of species known as the Triflora, characterized by their freely-produced, three-flower trusses, their small leaves and their upright, willow-like habit. *R. yunnanense* covers itself with pink, lavender or white flowers. Other similar species include: *R. davidsonianum*, pink flowers, usually spotted or blotched; *R. lutescens*, an early-flowered yellow with reddish new growth; *R. oreotrephes* , mauve-pink, purple, rose or white, with bluish leaves; and *R. rigidum* white. See *R. augustinii*, (p.49).

Hybrids

'Anna Baldsiefen'

Semi-dwarf/Low   H4   E–EM

A floriferous, dense and compact dwarf of upright habit with clusters of brightest pink flowers. Probably not for coldest areas as its flowers open rather early. Susceptible to rust fungus. A.M.T. 1979.

'Anna Rose Whitney'

Tall   H5   ML–L

A vigorous, large American hybrid with very bright, deep rose-pink flowers in rounded trusses. One of the hardiest hybrids of this colour. Needs to be pruned as a young plant, and rather susceptible to powdery mildew. A.M.T. 1987.

'Arctic Tern'

Low   H5   ML–L

An unusual hybrid which may be a hybrid between a rhododendron and a ledum. Flowers resemble the latter, white, very small but many to each rounded cluster. Small leaves on a vigorous, airy plant, best in full sun. Late flowering for a dwarf. A.M.T. 1984.

'Bashful'

Low   H5   M–ML

One of the hardiest *R. yakushimanum* hybrids. Rounded trusses of camellia-rose flowers, blotched deeper, which fade to off-white. Not particularly compact; leaves have no indumentum. Other similar 'yak' hybrids include '**Pink Cherub**' F.C.C.T. rose pink, paler in the centre, and '**Doc**', H.C. light pink, frilled flowers.

'Blue Diamond'

Low   H4–5   EM–M

One of the most popular of the small-leaved, purple-blue hybrids. Clusters of violet-blue flowers on a dense, upright grower. Leaves tend to spot in winter. Several clones exist. F.C.C. 1939. There are many other similar hybrids, the most common include: '**Blue Tit**' g., grey-blue flowers. Most clones have yellowish new growth and leaf spot, but some are good. '**Gristede**', better foliage, deep green and shiny, but with smaller violet-blue flowers. '**Penheale Blue**', F.C.C., wisteria-blue flowers and good foliage. '**St Breward**', F.C.C., '**St Tudy**', F.C.C.T., fine, large, bright, violet-blue flowers. Some leaf spotting.

'Blue Peter'

Medium   H5   M–ML

The most popular larger 'blue' hardy hybrid. Frilled, pale lavender flowers, flared purple, in a conical truss. Glossy leaves on a rather sprawling, untidy bush. F.C.C.T. 1958. **'A. Bedford'**, F.C.C.T., has a more upright growth habit, glossy leaves and red stems, and deeper lavender-mauve flowers, blotched purple.

'Carmen'

Dwarf/Semi-dwarf   H4   EM–M

Waxy, dark red flowers in loose, flat trusses, on a dense, spreading bush with small deep green leaves. Needs cool roots and good drainage. Best in drier gardens.

'Chionoides'

Low/Medium   H5   ML–L

One of the easiest to grow and toughest hybrids for general planting. Neat, rounded trusses of small, white flowers, with a yellow blotch. A dense, spreading grower tolerant of full exposure.

'Christmas Cheer'

Low/Medium   H5   E–EM

One of the most popular early flowering hybrids (it only opens at Christmas if forced). Blush-pink flowers with deeper stripes in tight, rounded trusses. The long-lasting flowers open over a long period, so even if some are frosted, others usually give a show. Easy to please, robust, hardy and versatile, and one of the best hardy hybrids for the beginner.

'Cilpinense'

Semi-dwarf/Low   H3–4   E

Trusses of pale, blush-pink flowers in clusters on a very free-flowering, easily grown, mounding plant with hairy leaves. Buds and flowers are not frost hardy, so not worth growing in gardens with the severest spring frosts. F.C.C. 1968. **'Snow Lady'**, very similar; pure white flowers with dark anthers. Hairier, more rounded leaves than the above.

'Crest'

Tall   H4   M–ML

One of the most popular yellow hybrids. Clear primrose-yellow flowers in an almost full, rounded truss. Deep green shiny leaves on a plant which tends to look sparse. Needs wind shelter but give plenty of light. Takes a few years to bud up. F.C.C. 1953.

'Cunningham's White'

Low/Medium   H5   ML–L

This is perhaps the most adaptable of all hybrids, being tolerant of pollution, neutral or slightly alkaline soil, wind and sun. Two clones seem to be in commerce, both have white flowers with

(Above) 'Curlew', *the most popular of the*
'bird' dwarf hybrids raised at Glendoick.

(Below) 'Cynthia', *a most popular old hardy*
hybrid. Grows very large in time.

yellow markings, but one has full rounded trusses while the other has less spectacular, looser trusses. Useful as a windbreak and background plant where *R. ponticum* is too invasive. Also popular as an understock for grafting.

'Curlew'

Dwarf   H4   EM–M

Relatively large, bright yellow flowers cover this dwarf hybrid raised in our own nurseries. Small green leaves on a plant which grows wider than tall. F.C.C.T 1986. Another of our own hybrids, **'Chikor'**, F.C.C., is smaller-growing with clusters of bright yellow flowers. A dense twiggy bush with tiny leaves. Needs good drainage, cool roots, and a little shade in warmer areas.

'Cynthia'

Tall   H5   ML–L

One of the most popular of the old hardy hybrids. Large domed trusses of rose-pink flowers, flushed magenta, spotted crimson. A vigorous grower which forms a very large bush. Reliable, free-flowering, hardy and easy to please. Somewhat susceptible to powdery mildew.

'Dopey'

Low   H4   M–ML

One of the best red 'yak' hybrids. Bright red flowers in full, rounded trusses. Dull green leaves, dusted silvery when young, on a rounded, compact plant.

Free flowering and easy to grow. F.C.C.T. 1979. **'Titian Beauty'**, deeper red flowers in smaller trusses. A more upright bush with deeper green leaves, thinly indumented below. These two are not as hardy as most of the pink 'yak' hybrids.

'Dora Amateis'

Semi-dwarf   H5   EM–M

A fine American hybrid with clusters of pure white flowers, flecked green. Pale green, small leaves on a spreading bush. Free flowering, hardy and reliable. F.C.C.T. 1981.

'Egret'

Dwarf   H4   M

A Glendoick hybrid with unusual, freely-produced, tiny, white bells. Small, shiny, deep green leaves on a compact plant. Best in the full sun. A.M.T. 1987.

'Elizabeth'

Low   H4   EM–M

The most popular medium-sized red hybrid for moderate gardens. Lax trusses of trumpet-shaped, bright red flowers. Long, pale green leaves on a bush of rounded habit, straggly in shade. Easy, free flowering and showy, but unfortunately very prone to powdery mildew. F.C.C. 1943. Its sister seedling **'Creeping Jenny'** has smaller flowers and a lower habit, and seems to be considerably less susceptible to mildew.

'Elizabeth Lockhart'

Semi-dwarf/Low   H4   EM–M

A very unusual hybrid, as it has rounded, reddish-purple leaves. A compact, dense grower which needs shade to preserve the leaf colour. Lax trusses of cherry-red, bell-shaped flowers. H.C.T. 1972.

'Fabia' g.

Low/Medium   H3–4   ML–L

Lax trusses of orange-red, orange, or salmon-pink flowers, depending on the clone. Lightly indumented leaves on a vigorous plant of loose habit. Needs wind shelter, but avoid too much shade. The most commonly available clone, 'Fabia', A.M., has orange-red flowers. 'Tortoiseshell' g. Later flowering, and less hardy than the above, best in milder gardens. The most popular clones are: 'Champagne', A.M., pale yellow, tinged pink; 'Orange', orange-red flowers; 'Wonder' A.M., salmon-pink.

'Fastuosum Flore Pleno'

Tall   H5   L

Long-lasting, semi-double, pale bluish-mauve flowers in loose trusses. Dull, convex leaves on an upright, vigorous, robust plant tolerant of sun and wind. One of the toughest hardy hybrids.

'Fragrantissimum'

Medium   H2   ML–L

Probably the most popular of the tender, scented hybrids. Loose trusses of white flowers, tinged pink and yellow, with a very strong scent. Has a deplorable straggly habit, and its long shoots need support from a wall, or it can be trained around stakes. Fine outdoors in mild areas, but usually grown as a conservatory plant. F.C.C. 1968. 'Lady Alice Fitzwilliam', F.C.C., is hardier, more compact, but with a less powerful scent. Both these hybrids are prone to rust fungus.

'Furnival's Daughter'

Medium   H4–5   ML–L

Pink flowers with a striking deeper red flare, in a tall truss. Tends to have poor roots and yellow foliage. F.C.C.T. 1961. 'Mrs Furnival', F.C.C.T., better foliage, but a smaller, more rounded truss. 'Mrs G.W. Leak', F.C.C.T., light rose-pink flowers with a brown and crimson flare. Tends to suffer from leaf spot.

'Ginny Gee'

Dwarf   H5   EM–M

One of the finest, recently introduced dwarfs. Clusters of pink and white flowers, giving a two-toned effect. A dense twiggy grower. Hardy, easy to please, and highly recommended. S.P.A. 1985.

'Golden Torch'

Low   H4   M–ML

Rounded trusses of pale, creamy-yellow flowers. A compact, dense grower, with healthy, deep green leaves, which can take a fair amount of exposure. The most popular 'yak' hybrid of this shade. A.M. 1984.

'Goldsworth Orange'

Medium   H4–(5)   L

Salmon-pink flowers with orange tones in flat-topped trusses. Upright in habit, but not over-vigorous. Flowers last best in some shade. Somewhat prone to powdery mildew. A.M. 1959.

'Gomer Waterer'

Medium   H5   L

White flowers, flushed mauve-pink, with a yellowish-brown flare. Thick, deep green leaves on a very tough, dense plant tolerant of wind and sun. A recommended hardy hybrid. A.M. 1906.

'Grace Seabrook'

Medium   H4   EM–M

One of the finest American hybrids. Large, fairly conical trusses of pure red. Deep green, pointed leaves on a vigorous plant. Rather early flowering for some gardens, but generally fairly tough. **'Taurus'** is very similar, but has red buds. **'David'**, F.C.C., fine red flowers on a bush of upright habit.

'Grumpy'

Semi-dwarf/Low   H5   M–ML

One of the neatest 'yak' hybrids. Very compact and dense, with indumented leaves. Flowers cream, flushed rose, opening slightly earlier than most 'yak' hybrids. A.M.T. 1979.

'Hoppy'

Low   H5   M–ML

Very frilly, lilac-pink flowers which fade to white. A fairly compact 'yak' hybrid with no indumentum under the leaves. A.M. 1977. **'Sleepy'** has pale phlox-purple flowers which fade to white, while **'Caroline Allbrook'** A.M., is slightly deeper purple.

'Hotei'

Medium   H4   M–ML

Named after a Japanese god, this has amongst the deepest yellow flowers of any hybrid. A dense grower, with medium-sized leaves. Needs wind shelter and very good drainage. A.M. 1974.

'Hummingbird' g.

Semi-dwarf   H(3)–4   EM–M

Cherry-red to rose, bell-shaped flowers in very lax trusses. Rounded leaves with a thin indumentum on a compact bush. Many clones exist, some of which are tender or have poor flowers.

'Hydon Dawn'

Low   H5   M–ML

A showy 'yak' hybrid with frilled, pale pink flowers, blotched deeper in the centre. Compact, with silvery tomentum on the leaves. Free flowering and hardy. A.M.T. 1986.

(Opposite) R. lindleyi, *one of the most spectactular tender scented species.*

'Intrifast'

Dwarf　　H5　　EM–M

A fine, compact, very low-growing hybrid with showy, small, glaucous-blue leaves. Clusters of violet-blue flowers. Hardy and reliable, best grown in full sun. 'Ramapo', fine grey-blue foliage on a compact, extremely hardy plant. Small pinkish-violet flowers. 'St Merryn', F.C.C.T., deep purple-blue flowers on a very low-growing plant. One of the best hybrids of this colour.

'Jean Marie de Montague'

Medium　　H4　　M

Rounded trusses of crimson-scarlet flowers. An upright but fairly slow-growing plant with thick leaves. One of the best of the Dutch red hybrids. 'Britannia', F.C.C.T., an old favourite with light red flowers and rather yellowy leaves. 'Kluis Sensation', a later-flowering, similar hybrid with fine scarlet flowers and pale, rather yellowish leaves.

'Lady Chamberlain' g.

Medium/Tall　　H3–(4)　　M

One of the many hybrids raised from the species *R. cinnabarinum* which passes on its clusters of pendulous waxy flowers to its offspring. 'Lady Chamberlain' has salmon-orange or orange-pink flowers (depending on the clone). Small leaves on an airy, upright bush. Needs wind shelter, and not for the coldest gardens. F.C.C. 1967. In common with *R. cinnabarinum* itself, its hybrids are very prone to powdery mildew which can defoliate or even kill plants (see p.105). Other similar hybrids include 'Lady Rosebery', F.C.C., pink flowers; 'Alison Johnstone', A.M., pale peachy-apricot flowers; 'Trewithen Orange', F.C.C., soft orange flowers, and 'Cinnkeys', A.M., orange and red tubular flowers.

'Lavender Girl'

Medium/Tall　　H5　　ML

Domed trusses of scented, pale lavender flowers. Glossy leaves on a tough, easily-grown plant, tolerant of sun and wind. F.C.C. 1967. 'Mrs Charles Pearson', F.C.C.T., pinkish-mauve flowers. Very hardy, but shy-flowering as a young plant. 'Susan', F.C.C.T., deeper flowers of bluish-mauve. Dark leaves are rounded at the ends. Somewhat prone to powdery mildew. Hard to root, so usually grafted.

'Lem's Monarch'

Tall　　H4　　M–ML

One of the newer, giant American hybrids. Huge conical trusses of white flowers rimmed with pink. Thick leaves on a sturdy, vigorous but fairly tidy grower. Best with some wind shelter.

'Linda'

Low　　H5　　EM

Frilled, rose-pink flowers in nearly full trusses. Egg-shaped pale green leaves on a compact, hardy, robust plant. A hybrid of the species *R. williamsianum*, which has been much used as a parent, and which passes on its pink flowers and rounded leaves to its offspring. There are many other good hybrids of this species; some of the most popular include: **'Bow Bells'**, loose trusses of pale-pink, bell-shaped flowers, and **'Gartendirektor Glocker'**, rosy-red, bell-shaped flowers.

'Loderi' g.

Tall   H3/4   M–ML

One of the most famous of all hybrids, over 30 different clones have been named from the cross. All the clones have large pale pink or white flowers in loose trusses and a beautiful scent. Long, rather pale leaves on a tree-like plant which takes a few years to flower. Not for coldest gardens, and needs wind-shelter and light shade. The most popular clones are **'Loderi King George'**, F.C.C., white, and **'Loderi Venus'**, light pink.

'Loder's White'

Medium/Tall   H4   M

Conical trusses of white flowers, tinged pink and spotted red. Good in sun or light shade, and easy to please. A.M. 1911. **'Beauty of Littleworth'**, F.C.C., huge trusses of white flowers, spotted red. A very large, ungainly grower.

'Markeeta's Prize'

Medium/Tall   H4   M

A fine American hybrid with rounded trusses of large, bright scarlet flowers.

Thick foliage on an upright, vigorous plant. **'Halfdan Lem'**, similar flowers which fade to cherry-red, on a vigorous, sometimes untidy bush. Flowers are amongst the largest available in this colour.

'Martha Isaacson'

Medium/Tall   H4–5   L

A very fine azaleodendron (azalea × rhododendron) raised in America. Lightly scented, white flowers with pink stripes. Semi-deciduous, reddish-bronze leaves which hang dejectedly in a hard winter.

'May Day' g.

Low/Medium   H3   M

Many different forms of this cross exist. Orange-red to red flowers in loose trusses. A fairly compact bush with indumented leaves. Not for coldest gardens. A.M. 1932. **'Matador'**, F.C.C., a taller-growing hybrid with darker red flowers. More tender than the above. **'Tally Ho'**, F.C.C., H2, late orange-scarlet flowers. Tender, really only suitable for mildest gardens.

'Moonstone' g.

Semi-dwarf/Low   H4   EM

Creamy yellow, bell-shaped flowers in loose trusses. Small oval leaves on a fairly compact plant. Early growth is prone to frost damage. **'Cowslip'** has very similar flowers, but with pink and red markings in the throat. A.M. 1937. **'Gartendirektor Rieger'**, from West

Germany, is hardier, later into growth and has larger leaves. Flowers cream, tinged rose, in loose trusses.

'Naomi' g.

Medium/Tall   H4–5   M

One of the famous Exbury hybrids. The various clones have fragrant flowers in nearly full trusses. Forms a small tree. Prone to powdery mildew. The most common clones are: **'Exbury'**, A.M., pale lilac and yellow; **'Nautilus'**, A.M., rose and pale orange frilled flowers.

'Nobleanum' g.

Medium   H4   VE–E

The earliest larger hybrid to flower. Many clones exist. Flowers can be bluish-scarlet, rose-red, pink or white. Leaves have thin indumentum below.

'Nova Zembla'

Medium   H5   ML–L

The most widely available, really hardy, red hybrid. Red flowers with a bluish tinge in rounded trusses. A sturdy upright plant, good in full exposure.

'Odee Wright'

Low/Medium   H4   M–ML

A fine American hybrid with full rounded trusses of primrose-yellow, pink-tinged flowers, spotted carmine in the throat. Deep green, glossy leaves on a slow-growing, compact plant. **'Carita'** g., a similar but more upright hybrid from Exbury; several clones exist.

'Carita A.M.**'** has pale primrose flowers, those of **'Inchmery'** are rose-pink and yellow, and **'Golden Dream'** has golden yellow flowers, fading to cream. **'Moonshine'** g., primrose-yellow flowers. Several clones exist. All above hybrids require some wind shelter.

'Patty Bee'

Dwarf   H5   EM

A fine, easily-grown dwarf. Relatively large, pale creamy-yellow flowers. A dense, compact grower. One of the

'Fabia'. There are not many orange rhododendrons, and this is one of the best.

hardiest dwarf yellows, but rather early into flower. s.p.a. 1985. **'Princess Anne'**, smaller flowers of a similar colour, later than the above. Bronzy young foliage, f.c.c.t. 1983.

'Percy Wiseman'

Low   H4–5   M–ML

A popular 'yak' hybrid with peach-pink and cream flowers in rounded trusses. Oval leaves have no indumentum below. A fairly compact, vigorous, sturdy plant. a.m.t. 1981.

'Fastuosum Flore Pleno'. This old favourite is one of the few double-flowered rhododendrons and is very hardy.

'Pink Drift'

Dwarf   H5   EM

A hardy, very dense and compact, free-flowering dwarf with very small leaves. Clusters of magenta-pink flowers. **'Wigeon'**, larger pinker flowers, on a compact plant with larger, grey-green leaves. a.m.t. 1987.

'Pink Pearl'

Tall   H4   ML–L

One of the most famous of all hybrids. Tall, conical trusses of soft pink flowers, fading to off-white. Upright and vigorous, with pale green leaves. f.c.c. 1900. **'Betty Wormald'**, f.c.c.t. less vigorous, and slightly deeper pink.

'**Mother of Pearl**', white flowers, flushed lavender-pink. A.M. 1930. '**Trude Webster**', deep pink flowers, fading to off-white. Thick foliage. S.P.A. 1971.

'**P.J. Mezitt/P.J.M.**'

Low   H5   E–EM

One of the hardiest hybrids ever raised, tolerating −32°C (−25°F). Rosy-purple flowers on a neat bush with small leaves, mahogany in winter. Best in full sun. Several clones exist.

'**Polar Bear**' g.

Tall   H4   VL

One of the latest-flowering of all hybrids. Loose trusses of scented, white flowers, spotted brown or green. Long, thin, pale green leaves on a vigorous grower which needs wind shelter. Flowers last best in light shade. F.C.C. 1946.

'**Praecox**'

Low/Medium   H4–5   E

A popular early-flowering hybrid. Rosy-purple flowers in small trusses. An upright grower with small leaves, which benefits from pruning. F.C.C. 1978. '**Bo Peep**', an early-flowering hybrid for milder areas. Clusters of pale greenish-yellow flowers. Susceptible to powdery mildew. A.M. 1934.

'**President Roosevelt**'

Medium   H4   M

One of the few variegated rhododendrons. Smooth green leaves have bold flashes of yellow variegation. These tend to revert, and green leaves should be removed. Bright red flowers, white in the centre. A rather floppy, brittle plant. '**Goldflimmer**', similar variegation to the above on a hardier, sturdier plant, which rarely reverts. Small trusses of mauve-pink flowers. '**Ponticum Variegatum**', narrow leaves are bordered with white variegation. Small trusses of mauve-pink flowers. Very easy to grow.

'**Ptarmigan**'

Dwarf/Semi-dwarf   H4   E

The Snow Grouse has somewhat frost-resistant, white flowers which open in batches over several weeks during milder, early spring weather. A spreading grower which forms a tangled mound. F.C.C. 1965.

'**Purple Splendour**'

Low/Medium   H4–5   ML–L

Spectacular, frilled, deepest purple flowers with a nearly black blotch in the centre. An upright bush, somewhat lacking in vigour. Somewhat susceptible to powdery mildew. A.M. 1931.

'**Razorbill**'

Semi-dwarf   H4   EM

Raised at Glendoick, this is becoming one of the most popular of all dwarf hybrids. Clusters of unusual, upward-pointing, tubular, pink flowers. A compact plant with crinkled leaves.

F.C.C.T. 1983. 'Seta', less hardy, earlier-flowering, and less compact than the above. Widely tubular flowers in clusters, light pink, striped deeper on the outside. Best in mild gardens. Susceptible to powdery mildew. F.C.C. 1960.

'Roseum Elegans'

Tall   H5   ML

The most commonly grown 'ironclad hybrid' for severest areas. Rounded trusses of rosy-lilac flowers on an upright but tidy bush. Very rugged and tolerant of sun and wind.

'Ruby Hart'

Low   H3–4   M

Very dark red flowers in lax trusses. Deep green ribbed leaves on a dense, compact plant. Not for coldest gardens. A.M. 1988.

'Sappho'

Tall   H5   ML–L

A very popular hardy hybrid with domed trusses of white flowers, strongly blotched black-purple. Dark, narrow leaves on a very vigorous plant which tends to sprawl untidily. A.M.T. 1974.

'Sarled'

Dwarf   H4   ML

An unusual hybrid with creamy white, daphne-like flowers in clusters. Tiny leaves on a very dense, compact dwarf. A.M. 1974. Late flowering for a dwarf. **'Maricee'**, A.E., A.M.T., taller growing

with white, peeling bark and similar but whiter flowers. Related species can be found under *R. trichostomum*.

'Scarlet Wonder'

Semi-dwarf/Low   H5   M

One of the most popular of all hybrids. Bright red, waxy flowers in loose trusses. Small, ribbed, oval leaves on a compact, dense plant which is extremely rugged. H.C.T., 1970. From the same cross are the very similar: **'Elisabeth Hobbie'** and **'Baden Baden'**. The latter has unusual twisted leaves.

'Scintillation'

Medium   H5   M–ML

A very hardy hybrid from eastern U.S.A. Pastel-pink flowers with a brown flare, in rounded trusses. Dark, glossy leaves on a sturdy bush. Best with a little wind protection. A.E. 1973.

'Seven Stars'

Low/Medium   H4–5   M–ML

One of the largest-growing and most spectacular 'yak' hybrids. Lightly scented, pale pink flowers, which fade to white, in large rounded trusses. Shiny, deep green leaves on a dense but upright plant. Rather prone to powdery mildew infection. F.C.C. 1974.

'Sir Charles Lemon'

Medium/Tall   H4   EM

One of the finest hybrids for foliage. Deep green, ribbed leaves have a striking cinnamon indumentum below, on a plant which forms a small tree. Pure white flowers in a domed truss. Best with some wind shelter.

'Sonata'

Low/Medium   H4–5   L

Small, open-topped trusses of orange flowers with claret centres. Smallish, matt, blue-green leaves on a dense, compact plant. One of the hardiest hybrids of this colour. H.C.T. 1959.

'Songbird'

Semi-dwarf   H4–5   EM

Clusters of deep violet-blue flowers. Small, glossy, deep green leaves on a dense, compact plant. A.M. 1957. 'Sacko', very similar but slightly later flowering. 'Azurwolke', less dense and with larger flowers and leaves.

'Surrey Heath'

Low   H4   M–ML

Two-toned flowers of pink and cream. A very compact 'yak' hybrid with pale leaves. A.M.T. 1982. 'Fantastica', a fine new German hybrid, hardier than the above, with two-toned flowers, red/pink shading inwards to white, in rounded trusses. 'Morgenrot', another German hybrid with rose-red flowers, fading to pale rose. Dark leaves with a thin indumentum below.

'Too Bee'

Dwarf   H4–5   EM

A fine new American hybrid with loose trusses of two-toned pink flowers. A very compact, dense grower. A.M. A sister seedling, 'Wee Bee', (syn. 'Not Too Bee') is slightly earlier into flower but is otherwise very similar.

'Unique'

Low/Medium   H4   EM/M

Cream flowers, flushed pink and yellow, in rounded trusses. A very dense compact plant, best in plenty of light. F.C.C. 1935. 'Bruce Brechtbill', identical in foliage and habit, but with pink flowers, flushed yellow. More striking in flower than 'Unique'.

'Vanessa Pastel'

Low/Medium   H3–4   ML

A very beautiful hybrid with lax trusses of deep cream flowers, shading to pink at the edges and stained red in the throat. A compact plant with narrow, pale green leaves. Not for cold gardens. F.C.C. 1971.

'Virginia Richards'

Medium/Tall   H4–5   M

A spectacular hybrid with two-toned flowers, rosy pink, fading to apricot-cream, blotched red in the throat. Deep green leaves on a vigorous but compact bush, best in full sun. One of the finest hybrids but unfortunately, susceptible to powdery mildew. A.M.T. 1985.

'Vulcan'

Medium   H5   L

Domed trusses of fiery blood-red flowers. Narrow leaves on a fairly vigorous bush. Hardy, but tends to produce frost-vulnerable growth late in the season. A.M.T. 1957.

'Whisperingrose'

Semi-dwarf   H4   EM

Relatively large, open bell-shaped, cherry-red flowers in lax trusses. Rounded, deep green leaves, bronzy when young, on a compact plant. Somewhat prone to powdery mildew.

'Winsome'

Low/Medium   H4   M–ML

Lax trusses of cherry-pink flowers. Dark pointed leaves, bronzy when young, on a compact, medium grower. Easy to please. A.M. 1950.

'Yellowhammer'

Medium   H4   EM–M

Masses of tiny, tubular, yellow flowers up the stems. Very small leaves on an upright bush which produces long shoots which can be pruned in flower for house decoration. Often flowers in autumn as well as spring.

□ **UNUSUAL HYBRIDS**

Dwarfs: Arctic Tern, Egret, Elizabeth Lockhart, Razorbill, Sarled.

Larger: Fastuosum, Flore Pleno, Lady Chamberlain, Marno Isaacson, President Roosevelt, Yellowhammer.

□ **SMALLER HYBRIDS:**
SOME CHOICES BY COLOUR

red	– 'Dopey', 'Elizabeth', 'Ruby Hart', 'Scarlet Wonder'
yellow	– 'Curlew', 'Chikor', 'Golden Torch', 'Patty Bee'
white	– 'Arctic Tern', 'Dora Amateis', 'Egret', 'Ptarmigan'
blue/purple	– 'Azurwolke', 'Blue Diamond', 'St Merryn'
pink	– 'Anna Baldsiefen', 'Ginny Gee', 'Fantastica', 'Linda'

□ **LARGER HYBRIDS:**
SOME CHOICES BY COLOUR

red	– 'Grace Seabrook', 'Jean Marie de Montague', 'Taurus',
yellow	– 'Crest', 'Hotei', 'Odee Wright', 'Yellowhammer'
white	– 'Chionoides', 'Loderi', 'Loder's White', 'Polar Bear'
blue/purple	– 'Blue Peter', 'Purple Splendour', 'Susan'
pink	– 'Lem's Monarch', 'Mrs Furnival', 'Vanessa Pastel'
orange/salmon	– 'Fabia', 'Goldsworth Orange', 'Sonata'

(Above) *'Hotei'. Raised in the U.S.A., this is one of the deepest yellow large-flowered hybrids.*

(Below) *'Lady Rosebery', one of the hybrids of R. cinnabarinum.*

> ☐ **HYBRIDS FOR SEVERE CLIMATES**
>
> 'Bashful', 'Fastuosum Flore Pleno', 'Gomer Waterer', 'Nova Zembla', 'P.J.M.', 'Ramapo', 'Roseum Elegans', 'Scarlet Wonder', 'Scintillation'

Deciduous Azaleas

These azaleas lose their leaves in autumn and winter so they may not be as useful in the landscape as their evergreen relations. Deciduous azaleas do, however, have certain features in their favour. Many have fine autumn colours, some have a fine scent, and some of the colours in the salmon-pink and orange shades are not available among the evergreen rhododendrons.

☐ SPECIES

R. calendulaceum

Medium   H4   ML–L

A fine, very hardy species from eastern U.S.A. with fiery orange and red flowers. A parent of many of the orange azalea hybrids. *R. prinophyllum*, from Canada and the U.S.A., has sweetly scented bright pink flowers and greyish or glaucous leaves.

R. luteum

Low/Medium   H4–5   M–L

This well-known plant from the Caucasus and eastern Europe has naturalized itself in parts of southern England. Yellow, sweetly-scented flowers. Leaves turn scarlet in autumn. Good in full exposure, but also shade-tolerant.

R. occidentale

Low/Medium   H4   L–VL

A western American species with sweetly-scented flowers, white flushed yellow and/or pink. Many different forms exist. Useful for its late flowering. *R. viscosum*, from the eastern seaboard of the U.S.A. Fragrant, white to pinkish flowers. Also late-flowering. Known as the 'swamp honeysuckle' and likes moist conditions.

R. schlippenbachii

Low/Medium   H4   M

Perhaps the finest deciduous azalea species in flower. Large pink or white flowers. Large leaves for an azalea, rounded at the ends. Tends to grow early, so needs shelter in severer gardens. *R. albrechtii* has smaller flowers, usually bright rose-purple. Also tends to grow early.

☐ HYBRIDS

Deciduous azalea hybrids exist in many shades. Seedlings of the hybrid strains such as Mollis and Exbury are usually available by colour and are fine for massed plantings. Deciduous azalea hybrids are generally tough, most are hardy to −23°C (−10°F) or colder. There are several hybrid groups, named after either the parents used or the place

'*Linda*', *a showy, reliable, low-growing Dutch hybrid ideal for the beginner.*

they were originally raised. In the northern hemisphere, they flower in May and June, starting with the Mollis hybrids. The hybrid group which each variety belongs to is designated by the letters in parentheses following the clonal naming. The categories are:

Ghent (Gh)
The oldest hybrids, raised in Belgium. Small flowers, often in pastel colours. Tall growing. A few are scented. Good autumn colour.

Mollis (Mo)
Quite low-growing, with medium-sized flowers. The earliest-flowering group in shades of red, yellow, orange and pink.

Knaphill/Exbury (Kn)
The largest flowers and the brightest colours; red, orange, pink, salmon, cream, white and combinations of these. Some clones have large, full, rounded trusses and some are scented.

Occidentale (Oc)
Paler flowers, pink, yellow and white, usually strongly scented.

There are hundreds of deciduous azalea hybrids; most are perfectly good. The following is a selection of the most common ones.

'Berryrose', A.M. (Kn)	Salmon-pink, marked red, yellow throat. Coppery young growth.
'Brazil' (Kn)	Bright tangerine-orange and red, frilled flowers.
'Cecile' (Kn)	Full trusses of large, salmon-pink flowers, yellow throat.
'Coccinea Speciosa' (Gh)	Masses of tangerine and red flowers giving an effect like honeysuckle.
'Daviesii' (Gh)	Pale yellow, pink and white flowers. Sweetly scented. Low-growing.
'Fireball' (Kn)	Orange-red, with yellow stamens. Coppery-red young growth.
'Gibraltar' (Kn)	The most popular hybrid. Frilled, crinkled, orange-red flowers, yellow in the throat, in a large, full truss.
'Glowing Embers' (Kn)	Orange-red. Compact.
'Golden Sunset', A.M. (Kn)	Light yellow, tinged orange, flared orange in the throat.
'Homebush', A.M.T. (Kn/Gh)	Pompom-like ball-shaped trusses of semi-double carmine-pink flowers. Unusual and very popular.

'Hotspur', A.M. (Kn)	Orange-red, flared yellow.
'Irene Koster' (Oc)	White, flushed crimson and pink, flared yellow. Strongly scented.
'Klondyke' (Kn)	Deep, golden-yellow flowers, salmon-pink on reverse. Coppery new growth.
'Persil' (Kn)	Large pure white flowers, blotched yellow.
'Royal Command' (Kn)	Orange-red, fading to yellow. Good autumn colour.
'Satan' (Kn)	Geranium-red.
'Silver Slipper', F.C.C.T. (Kn)	Fragrant, creamy-white flowers, flared yellow, tinged pink. Bronze new growth.
'Strawberry Ice', A.M.T. (Kn)	Large, full trusses, flesh-pink, flushed deeper, yellow throat.

Evergreen Azaleas

Bred in the U.K., Europe, Japan, the U.S.A and elsewhere, there are hundreds of fine hybrids now commercially available. The colour range includes red, pink, salmon, white and reddish-purple (and intermediates). The 'Satsuki' azaleas from Japan sometimes have several flower colours on one bush. These are only suitable for hot climates. Evergreen azalea flowers are sometimes double, semi-double or hose-in-hose (one flower inside another). Most grow well in milder and/or hotter climates, such as in parts of southern England, western France, Italy, south-east and western U.S.A. and elsewhere. In colder, cooler and more northern climates only certain varieties are successful. These are noted in the text.

The following is a selection of the most commonly offered species and hybrids. Most flower late midseason (late in May in the U.K.) Some are a week or two later. Taller growing varieties can eventually get to 1 m (3¼ ft) in favourable conditions. The lowest growers creep along the ground, below 15 cm (6 in) in height. Flower size ranges in diameter from 1–8 cm (⅜–3 in). As a general rule the smaller-flowering varieties produce such a profusion of bloom that they are just as showy as their larger-flowered relatives. They are largely trouble-free and easy plants, but they do sometimes suffer from gall fungus (see p.104).

'Addy Wery', A.M.	Vermilion-scarlet. Early-flowering, tall and upright.

(Opposite) *'Pink Pearl', one of the most popular hybrids ever raised but, beware, it eventually gets very large.*

'Amoenum'

Very old Chinese hybrid. Hose-in-hose, rosy-purple. Low, spreading habit.

'Beethoven'

Large, lilac-mauve flowers.

'Blaauw's Pink'

Hose-in-hose, salmon-pink. Early.

'Blue Danube', F.C.C.T.

Fine, fairly large, bluish-violet flowers. Tender in coldest areas.

'Diamant'

Low-growing German hybrids, available in several shades, including red, pink, white and lilac. Excellent in severest climates.

'Favourite'

Rosy-pink. Dense grower. Early.

'Hatsuguri', F.C.C.T.

Magenta. Low, spreading. Semi-deciduous.

'Hino Crimson', H.C.T.

Bright crimson. For milder areas. Reddish leaves in winter.

'Hinodegiri', A.M.T.

Bright red, early. Medium height.

'Hinomayo', F.C.C.T.

Bright, phlox-pink. Semi-deciduous.

'Johanna', A.M.

Carmine red. Fine foliage. Hardy.

'John Cairns', A.M.T.

Fairly large, indian-red flowers. Quite tall-growing, but dense. Bronzy winter colour.

'Kermesina'

Very hardy, one of the best for cold and northern gardens. Bright pink, compact.

'Kermesina Rose'

Pink and white, striped flowers. Very hardy, compact. Newly introduced.

'Kirin', A.M.T.

For milder gardens. Very attractive hybrid; bicolour pink flowers.

R. kiusianum

A hardy Japanese species, good in northern climates. Very compact. Many forms exist with flowers of purple, red, pink, salmon or white. More or less deciduous.

'Lemur'

One of our own hybrids. Deep pink, long-lasting flowers on a compact spreader.

'Leo'

Large, salmon-orange flowers. Late. Low, spreading habit.

'Mother's Day', F.C.C.T.

Large, crimson flowers. Low, spreading. Leaves bronzy in winter. Prone to galls.

'Mucronatum', A.M.

Large, white flowers. Upright-growing with hairy leaves.

R. nakaharae

Late-flowering, Taiwanese species. Very dwarf, creeping or mounded habit. Red or salmon-red flowers. Good in Scotland.

'Orange Beauty', F.C.C.T.

Salmon-orange. Low-growing. Early.

'Palestrina', F.C.C.

Large, white flowers. Upright growing. Some clones are hardier than others.

'Panda'

One of our own hybrids. White flowers. Low growing. Hardy. Good in Scotland.

'Rosebud', A.M.T.

Double pink flowers. Late. Very compact. Not for the coldest gardens.

'Squirrel'

Bright scarlet. Fairly late. Compact. One of our hybrids. Good in Scotland.

'Vida Brown', A.M.T.

Large hose-in-hose, deep salmon-pink flowers. Very compact and slow-growing with small leaves.

'Vuyk's Rosy Red', F.C.C.T.

Large rosy-red flowers. Not completely hardy in Scotland, but very popular in England and elsewhere.

'Vuyk's Scarlet', F.C.C.T.

The most popular azalea in the U.K. Crimson flowers. Early. Low and spreading. Hardy.

'Willy'

Rosy-pink. Semi-deciduous. Good in colder gardens.

'Wombat'

A carpeter with bright pink flowers. Good in Scotland.

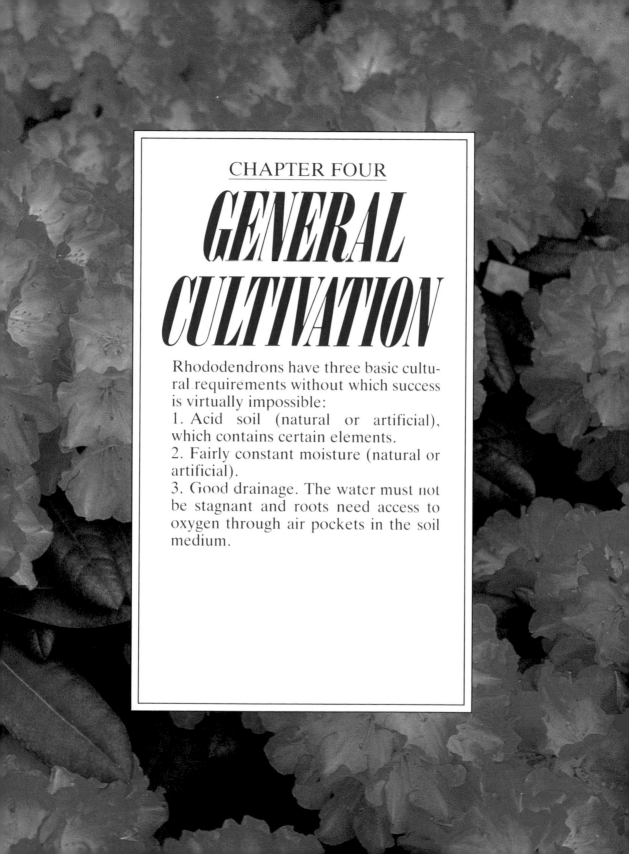

CHAPTER FOUR

GENERAL CULTIVATION

Rhododendrons have three basic cultural requirements without which success is virtually impossible:

1. Acid soil (natural or artificial), which contains certain elements.

2. Fairly constant moisture (natural or artificial).

3. Good drainage. The water must not be stagnant and roots need access to oxygen through air pockets in the soil medium.

SOILS

pH is the term used to measure the acidity or alkalinity of soil. pH 7.0 is neutral, higher than 7.0 is alkaline, lower is acid. Most soils are neutral or acid; alkaline ones are generally found in areas of limestone and chalk. Rhododendrons generally require a soil of pH 4.5–6.0. The relationship between rhododendron health, the minerals they need and soil pH is very complex.

One major factor concerns the high calcium content of limy soil. Rhododendrons need very little calcium, but on limy soil, they take up large quantities of it, causing poisoning. In addition, high pH tends to 'lock up' elements necessary for the healthy growth of rhododendrons; this is particularly true in the case of iron. Soil pH is easily measured, using a home soil test kit; alternatively several organizations offer a soil testing service.

You can generally get an adequate idea of the pH of your locality by looking to see what your neighbours are growing in their gardens. Healthy rhododendrons, camellias, heathers and other acid lovers indicate suitable soil. Conversely, no acid lovers indicates alkaline soil (or a neighbourhood of rhododendron haters!). Even if your local soil is acid, vegetable growing or recent building often results in areas of limy soil in gardens, and testing may be necessary to find out if this is so.

If your soil is really alkaline, (pH 8.0 or above) then it is very unlikely that you will be able to grow rhododendrons at all, except in containers, irrigating with rain or chemically treated water, as local water will almost certainly be alkaline. In more neutral soils, raised beds can be made, isolated with polythene from the original garden soil if necessary, for planting smaller-growing varieties. If the soil is only slightly alkaline, the pH can be lowered by adding peat, composted bark, leaf-mould and other acid substances. Sulphur can be used as an acidifier; this is best applied as ammonium sulphate or flowers of sulphur. Avoid aluminium sulphate. Fritted trace elements may also be needed to supply any elements missing from the soil. Sequestrenes (chelates), which are sold as a rhododendron soil-acidifier and as a provider of iron can help, but they are expensive and they occasionally damage sensitive species.

Another option for those with neutral or slightly acid soil is to choose species and hybrids which tolerate near neutral soils. Some of the best include: *R. augustinii*, *R. decorum*, *R. hirsutum*, *R. rubiginosum*, *R. vernicosum* and 'Cunningham's White'. Plants grafted onto 'Cunningham's White' also show greater tolerance of alkaline conditions. The best advice for people on neutral or alkaline soil who want to grow rhododendrons (apart from 'moving house') is to ask neighbours who have healthy rhododendrons which varieties they are and what planting techniques have been used.

□ ORGANIC MATTER
Rhododendrons need a well-aerated soil rich with organic matter (peat, acid

'Purple Splendour', the deepest purple large-flowered hybrid.

leafmould, conifer needles, composted bark, and other similar materials). A woodland soil rich with rotted leaves is ideal, while heavy clay is the worst. Most people have soil somewhere between these two extremes, and thorough soil preparation is always worthwhile. A rough test of soil drainage is to dig a hole of the correct planting depth and fill it with water. The more slowly the water drains away, the more the drainage needs improving. Soil consistency is quite easy to gauge by picking up a handful and squeezing it. If it is spongy and only partly crumbles, then it probably contains a sufficient proportion of organic matter. If it can be compressed into a dense mass, then it probably contains a high proportion of clay. Sandy soil very readily crumbles into small particles; such soils usually drain exceptionally well, and they benefit from additions of organic matter to help conserve moisture. It is always better to plant in soil which drains too well than in one which doesn't drain well enough. The ground can always be watered in dry conditions, but soil which suffers waterlogging during the growing season cannot sustain healthy rhododendrons.

Rhododendrons need organic matter for several reasons. The most important is that it allows the simultaneous access of moisture and air to the roots. This is the fundamental requirement for rhododendron cultivation. In addition, the composting or decomposing of these materials generally acidifies the soil and ' releases most of the elements which rhododendrons need to grow healthily.

Organic materials which are partially decomposed are most suitable; fresh materials require nitrogen from the soil to break down, thus competing for it with the rhododendrons. At Glendoick, we rake up piles of leaves and allow them to break down for a year before using them in a compost or planting mixture.

Obviously, not everyone has access to leafmould, and for most people, peat is the most easily available organic material. Peat is a scarce resource, and its widespread use is causing the destruction of wetland habitats in many parts of the world. Peat bogs are thousands of years old and grow at a rate of as little as 1mm (0.04in) a year, so there is no hope of replacing them as they are used up. Peat is important in commercial rhododendron production, but is not always a particularly efficient organic material in the garden, as it is already very well decomposed and is often too fine to aerate the soil well. It is also very hard to wet after it dries out. The best coarse peat is now hard to obtain, and much of what is sold isn't worth its price. For an ideal planting medium try to obtain coarse peat and mix it with your own topsoil, and with other organic materials if you can obtain them.

Composted tree-bark is gradually receiving more and more favour as a major planting material for rhododendrons. It is particularly good for improving drainage and is especially useful in containers; we are using it more and more at Glendoick. As a by-product of the timber industry, it is far more environment-friendly than peat. In some areas, coarse sawdust may be available, but avoid using the fine sawdust commonly available in the U.K. Sawdust requires the addition of nitrogen to help in its breakdown.

Many other materials, as long as they are not alkaline or toxic, make a good addition to a growing medium. Try waste products from agriculture in small quantities on a few plants first, and if they work, then incorporate them into your soil. People have successfully used sweet corn husks, spent hops, brown (dead) bracken fronds, and even household rubbish such as newspaper and cardboard for this purpose. Don't use uncomposted grass cuttings.

There are several alternative strategies for sites with heavy clay soil. Some sort of drainage can be attempted, either by open or tile drains. Alternatively the soil can be broken up by ploughing, rotovating or digging, left to freeze to break it up, and then other materials can be added. Acid sand is a good material, if you can get it, as it lasts indefinitely, but it is very heavy to work with and is generally expensive. Bark is a good alternative. Gypsum (calcium sulphate), sprinkled onto the surface, will flocculate the clay (break it into small particles). The other option is to make raised beds of imported materials above the natural soil level, perhaps adding a small percentage of the original soil.

Rhododendrons can be either planted in individual holes or in prepared beds. Individual holes are fine for large-growing rhododendrons in a woodland garden, or for planting among established rhododendrons or other trees and shrubs. Dig a hole considerably larger than the rootball to allow several years' root-growth into prepared soil, and add plenty of organic matter. Prepared beds are better for dwarfs and for azaleas, and for planting in lawns or areas of rough grass where the grass would soon grow around the rootball if individual holes were dug. In preparing beds, fork or dig in organic matter through the whole bed. Wooden planks or peat blocks can be used to give different levels, or for terracing on a slope. Overall, the importance of good soil preparation cannot be stressed enough; dense, vigorous, healthy-leaved, free flowering rhododendrons should result.

MULCHING

The organic matter in the soil slowly breaks down and requires replacing. In woodland conditions, the leaves of trees and the rhododendrons' own leaf-litter give a good natural supply of organic materials, but of course many gardens do not have this luxury. If you have no natural leaf fall, it is very beneficial to apply a mulch or root dressing of some organic material when planting, and to repeat this every year or two afterwards. Peat is generally not very suitable for this as it tends to dry out, and then sheds water, or blows away. Leafmould, bark, wood chips, conifer needles and any of the other substances mentioned previously (or a mixture of them) make fine mulching materials. Do not use uncomposted grass cuttings as they will heat up, killing the rhododendron roots.

☐ **WHY MULCH?**

1. Retains and adds organic matter to the soil
2. Controls weeds around the roots
3. Retains moisture by preventing evaporation
4. Checks erosion of soil protecting roots, especially on a sloped planting
5. Helps protect roots from heat in summer and frost in winter
6. Looks attractive (especially bark)

In spite of all these favourable attributes, there are some rhododendron experts who do not recommend mulching, as they claim that it prevents water getting to the roots. In fact, as long as materials such as peat and sawdust, which form an impervious mat, are not used on their own, this is not generally a problem. In some climates mulches may encourage root weevils and other pests. Despite these occasional shortcomings, as a general rule, the benefits of mulching far outweigh any shortcomings.

FERTILIZER

In ideal conditions, with a soil rich in organic matter, fertilizer is rarely necessary. If your rhododendrons produce adequate growth with healthy, deep green foliage, and they flower freely, it is not necessary to give them extra feeding. Most of us have less than ideal conditions, and some fertilizer is of benefit. Starved rhododendrons show the condition by the general yellowing of their leaves or by interveinal chlorosis (the veins of the leaves remain green while the rest of the leaf turns yellow). Chlorosis is a common indicator of unhappy rhododendrons, caused by wrong soil pH, excess water, over-deep planting or poor drainage, as well as showing a need for fertilizer.

Compound fertilizers contain three main ingredients: nitrogen (N) for growth and healthy foliage, and phosphate (P) and potash/potassium (K) for ripening wood and production of flower-buds. The analysis of fertilizers is given using the formula N.P.K., and fertilizers with fairly low nitrogen content are desirable. Try to find a fertilizer with a formula of N12:P6:K6 or thereabouts (the formula will be given on the fertilizer container). Most importantly, ensure that the nitrogen is in the form of ammonia rather than as nitrates. Nitrate fertilizers of the type used for vegetables and cereals release large quantities of nitrogen very quickly, and this will burn most rhododendrons and can be fatal. Nitrate fertilizers include the Growmore types. The ammonia in fertilizers suitable for rhododendrons usually takes the form of ammonium sulphate, which has the added bonus of being a soil acidifier. Organic fertilizers such as hoof and horn and seaweed extracts can also be used, but beware of farmyard manure. Only use it if it is very well-rotted, and preferably well mixed with other substances.

Fertilizers with nitrogen should only be applied from spring to midsummer. Nitrogen applied later than this will cause soft late growth, discourage flower buds from being formed and prevent the plant ripening its wood sufficiently to withstand the winter. In general, larger hybrids and deciduous azaleas respond best to applications of fertilizer. Some dwarfs and larger species resent fertilizer and will have their leaves burned by it. If in doubt, give low applications, perhaps three times during the growing season, watching out for leaf burn. For larger hybrids and deciduous azaleas, compound fertilizer can be applied at a rate of 33g/sqm (1oz/sqyd). Scatter the fertilizer over the surface of the rootball as far as the drip line. The best overall advice for fertilizers is to use them with care and moderation, particularly on prized plants.

PLANTING

Unlike many plants, rhododendrons can be planted at any time of the year, even in full flower, due to their compact fibrous rootballs. Having said this, it is certainly advisable to do most planting during the autumn or early spring, before growth starts. The reasoning behind this is that the fibrous rootball must be in very good contact with the surrounding soil to take up sufficient moisture and nutrients to grow really healthily. By planting in autumn or early spring, rain and snow will have washed soil well around the rootball, and the plant will be able to start pushing fresh roots out into the soil at the beginning of the growing season, before the hottest and driest weather

starts. There is no reason why rhododendrons planted in late spring or summer should not grow perfectly well, and not surprisingly, many people do like to buy their rhododendrons from garden centres and nurseries in flower, so they know exactly what they're getting. But these plants must not be allowed to dry out during their first growing season. Overall, the best tactic is to do all really major planting in the dormant months and just buy small quantities of plants during the late spring and summer, which can have extra attention once planted in the garden.

Beware of buying plants in early spring that have their growth far-advanced due to their having been grown in a more favourable area than your own, or in a tunnel-house, or because the spring has been particularly mild. Don't plant out rhododendrons in growth until frost danger is passed. If the variety has frost-vulnerable flowers, it is worth keeping it inside as a houseplant until later in the season, but don't keep it in a hot, dry room. Alternatively, keep plants in their containers under cover for a while, or plant them and protect them with cloches, sacking, etc., during frost.

Rhododendrons must not be planted too deeply. They are essentially surface-rooting plants, and the top of the rootball should be only just under the soil. Most rhododendrons will die if planted too deeply, especially in areas of high rainfall. Don't mound soil up around the stem, and don't trample the earth over the rootball too hard. There is no point in putting fertilizer at the bottom of a rhododendron hole, as is commonly done with other plants, since rhododendrons are surface feeders. Use fertilizer sparingly at planting time, sprinkled onto the surface before watering in. As stated previously, holes should be prepared by digging in organic matter in an area considerably larger than the rootball. If the rootball has become very pot-bound (it completely fills the pot and new growth is being or has been clearly restricted), it will benefit from having the roots carefully teased outwards so that they can make good soil contact. I have dug up many unhappy plants after a year or two and found a very obvious pot-shape to be still visible, indicating that the roots have never managed to grow successfully into the surrounding soil.

If a rootball is dry, give it a really good soaking before planting by dunking the plant for a while in a bucket or sink. The peaty compost in most rhododendron containers repels water once it gets dry, and no amount of rain water will penetrate a really dry rootball. In all rhododendron and azalea planting, the soil should be firmly pressed around the EDGE of the rootball to ensure root-soil contact. Do NOT stamp on TOP of the rootball. This simply pushes the plant too deep and compresses the soil below the rootball, spoiling the drainage. After planting, rhododendrons and azaleas should be well watered-in to ensure that the feeding roots make good contact with the surrounding soil. It is better to plant in fairly dry conditions wherever possible, as most soil becomes sticky and glutinous if worked when

wet. Tall or top heavy plants may need staking for a year or two.

On a slope, or in very well drained

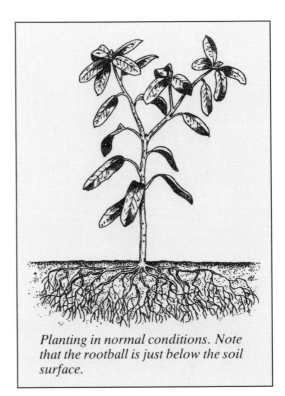

Planting in normal conditions. Note that the rootball is just below the soil surface.

soil, a saucer-shaped depression may be necessary to collect sufficient moisture for the roots, and to hold on to a mulch.

In the wettest gardens, or with varieties needing the best drainage, mound-planting can be used. The base of the rootball should be at or just below ground level, and the planting medium should be built up above this. Care must be taken that the roots always remain covered, and that soil is prevented from blowing away.

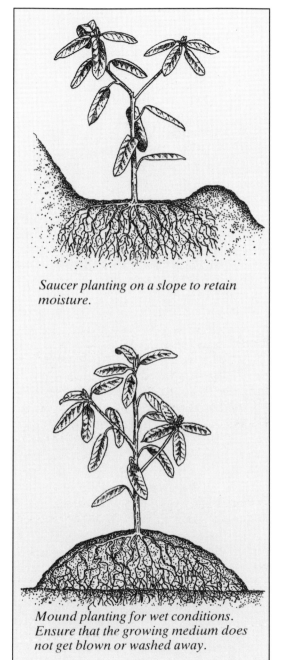

Saucer planting on a slope to retain moisture.

Mound planting for wet conditions. Ensure that the growing medium does not get blown or washed away.

□ MOVING PLANTS

Rhododendrons are generally quite easily moved, most even in full flower and at considerable age. This allows rhododendrons to be planted quite close together for instant effect, and to be thinned out later. Hardy hybrids, dwarfs and evergreen azaleas grow most healthily and look best in dense plantings with few spaces between them, and there is no great need to thin these out as they fill in.

Many other varieties of rhododendrons (particularly species) do, however, look best if they can grow outwards and upwards unhindered, and this often means moving large plants about. In addition, horrendous colour clashes, mistakes in site selection, and moving house can all result in a desire to move plants. Some people have managed successfully to take entire rhododendron collections with them through several moves of house. Plants up to 6 × 6m (20 × 20ft) have been moved with cranes perfectly successfully; size is really no problem, provided you have the means to do the digging and the moving. Obviously the more rootball you can take with the plant the better, but usually you can reduce it considerably without too much harm being done.

If you end up with a disproportionately small rootball, you can reduce the size of the top somewhat to compensate (see pruning p.98). The roots of a rhododendron generally extend to about 50% of the plant's foliage diameter, although this is a very rough estimate; it can be far more or much less. The roots are usually less than 45 cm (18 in) deep, even on a very large plant.

To move a large plant, start digging around the plant quite far out from the stem, and continue towards it until you meet roots. Then dig all round underneath the rootball (be careful, many a spade has come to grief doing this!), gently rocking the plant to ease the rootball from the soil. Watch out when lifting a plant by its main stem; it may not be strong enough to carry the weight of the rootball. The root can best be reduced by prising soil from it with a fork, rather than by slicing off roots and soil simultaneously with a spade. The plant can be barrowed or dragged short distances, or rootballed with polythene, burlap or other material for a longer distance move.

A rhododendron can remain out of the ground for considerable periods if you keep frost and sun from the roots, and ensure that it receives regular watering. Heeling it into the ground, or covering the roots with peat, leafmould or other materials usually gives adequate protection. Although rhododendrons can be moved during the growing season, they will require extra watering after transplanting if they are moved in growth. Evergreen and deciduous azaleas do not move well once they are in growth, so these should only be transplanted in autumn and winter.

WATERING

Some sheltered woodland gardens rich in organic matter rarely need watering at all (and often cannot be watered anyway). Unfortunately, most growers do not have such fortunate circumstances, and their soil will dry out from time to time. Rhododendrons and azaleas require fairly constant moisture in the soil during the growing season, but do not like to be overwatered; indeed overwatering coupled with poor drainage is a killer for most varieties. Young and newly-planted rhododendrons, and specimens near to or under greedy trees and shrubs, require the most extra watering. Rhododendrons wilt visibly when they are dry, so the problem is easy to spot. Don't panic if you notice this; the leaf cells contract as they dry out, and in addition, the plant has a natural response to lessen the leaf surface-area for evaporation of water by curling up the leaves. This happens in hot, dry and frosty weather, and rhododendrons will generally recover from it perfectly, so long as this condition is not allowed to persist for too long. Rhododendrons in flower need fairly constant moisture to prevent the flowers wilting, but beware of watering overhead, it can bruise paler flowers and cause petal blight (see p.105).

The early summer, after flowering, when the main flush of growth appears, is the most important time for moisture. Dry conditions will give less lush, shorter growths, and if really dry the plant will not grow at all. Good mulching will slow down evaporation and so lessen the need for extra watering. Watering can be done by hand in a small garden, or with sprinklers or trickle/seep hoses. It is better to give a more occasional really good soaking than regular light sprinklings. In some parts of the world, especially in western America, permanent sprinkler systems are often installed throughout the garden. Such systems produce very good growth, but beware if there is any risk of water restrictions; reduce watering gradually if drought is threatened. If your water is alkaline, use rainwater if possible; some artificial water softeners harm rhododendrons, so test them carefully.

Dwarf rhododendrons and evergreen azaleas generally tolerate drier conditions than larger species and hybrids, so are probably the best choice for dry gardens where artificial watering is impossible. Late on during the summer, dry conditions are actually beneficial to rhododendrons, as they encourage a good bud-set for the following year and stop the plant growing in good time to harden off for the winter. Artificial watering should be tapered off during this period.

WEEDS

Due to their shallow roots, rhododendrons and azaleas hate weeds, particularly grass, growing over their rootballs. In the wild, rhododendrons generally grow in colonies, as dwarf mats at high altitudes, and as thickets, groups or forests lower down the mountains. The resulting rhododendron canopy prevent vigorous weeds and other shrubs being able to grow over the roots. The same tactic can be used in cultivation by planting rhododendrons in groups, and allowing plants to grow

into one another. Where individual specimens are grown, mulching will help to prevent weed build-up.

In a woodland garden or other informal planting, weeds are not usually intrusive until after the main flowering season, when they can simply be scythed to keep them in check. In a small garden, hand-weeding is the most desirable approach. Try not to walk over your rhododendron beds while doing this as it compresses the soil over the roots, which rhododendrons hate. Use stepping stones in large beds, or use a hoe. The latter should be used with care, as rhododendron roots are so near the soil surface. If you have to remove a bad weed infestation by hand, be careful not to leave the rhododendron roots uncovered by removing too much soil with the weeds.

For a new planting site, removal of all or most weeds is desirable. When planting a bed in a lawn, the grass should be sprayed out with glyphosate or paraquat during the growing season, and left for several months before planting. Dead grass roots make a good planting medium as long as the sprayed-out bed is thoroughly dug over. Extra organic matter should be added before planting. If planting in rough ground, brambles, cleavers and other vigorous broad-leaved weeds will need to be eradicated. Glyphosate sprayed during the growing season is perhaps the most effective total weedkiller. Don't let it drift on to valuable plants – it kills anything with green leaves or shoots. Planting can begin ten weeks or so after application. Sodium chlorate is also very effective, but it remains active in the ground for at least six months after use.

The legislation surrounding these total (and therefore potentially very dangerous) weedkillers is constantly being tightened, and several effective weedkillers have now, quite rightly, been banned, because of their residual effect on the environment, and their toxicity to humans and animals. Total weedkillers can be applied with knapsack sprayers and watering cans. Always be careful of drift on to other plants, and of the fumes given off by some weedkillers, which can distort growth.

For spraying around established rhododendrons to keep the root-area weed-free, paraquat is very effective. It is harmless on woody stems, but drops of spray on green rhododendron stems and foliage will cause leaf-spotting. Paraquat can be applied two to three times a year. Some weeds, including nettles, are unfortunately fairly resistant to it. A granular pre-emergence (preventive) weedkiller (dichlobenil) can be used effectively on most rhododendrons, although there are a few varieties which resent it. Do not use a pre-emergence weedkiller on deciduous azaleas or on deciduous rhododendrons such as *R. camtschaticum*.

PRUNING AND PINCHING

Rhododendrons do not need regular pruning, but they do often benefit from some cutting back to improve shape and habit. Dead wood should be removed during the winter, as it encourages disease. Some varieties are naturally dense and compact and rarely need any pruning at all, while others are lanky and branch poorly. If rhododendrons are in too much shade, or are growing in an overcrowded situation, cutting them back is often the only way to obtain attractive plants. This scenario often occurs in old or neglected gardens. A few larger species such as *R. thomsonii*, *R. falconeri*, *R. sinogrande* and *R. macabeanum* do not respond well to this sort of treatment, but most other rhododendrons and azaleas will sprout from pruned branches to some extent.

Prune back a portion at a time, and wait until fresh sprouting is seen before continuing. Tidy up stumps above where the buds have sprouted. Some green leaves should always be left to allow the plant to photosynthesize. Don't prune during late summer, as this encourages vigorous, soft growth which may not harden in time for the winter. It is also important to remember that rhododendrons flower on the previous season's wood, so if you prune in the autumn or winter, you will be removing any flower buds which have already formed. One solution is to cut for the house when in flower, cutting back to the previous season's growth at the same time. Overall, the best time to prune is in early summer, just after flowering. On a poor straggly specimen, it is of course worth losing a year's flowers for the resulting improvement in shape. You cannot generally prune a rhododendron bush to keep it small. It may work once, but it is usually easier to move plants, or to start again if they get too large.

'Razorbill'. This unusual dwarf was raised at our own nursery at Glendoick.

Larger-leaved (elepidote) rhodo-dendrons produce growth shoots with whorls or rosettes of leaves at the end. At the centre of the rosette there is either a leaf or flower bud. Surrounding this central bud is the circle of leaves; each leaf has a bud just above it which has the potential to produce a new shoot. Where flower buds are produced, several axillary or side buds will usually sprout automatically after flowering is finished. Where there has been no flower-bud, as is common in young plants, often only the single growth-bud will have sprouted, and this can be pruned off to encourage side-branching. A bush which has never been pruned may have branches similar to the following:

Pruning to improve shape. A typical branch which can be pruned at any of the points 'A', 'B' or 'C'.

This can be pruned at any of the points 'A', 'B', or 'C', in most varieties. At point 'C' the rosette of leaves has dropped off, but the buds are still there. These may be covered by bark, but will still be discernible as small bumps. There is usually a visible circular mark or scar around the branch, indicating where the rosette was. Cut just above this. Having pruned the bush, several shoots should sprout, giving a more dense, compact shape to your plant.

This technique can also be used as a preventive measure to encourage bran-ching, and therefore to form denser, tidier, more compact bushes. This is known as 'pinching'. Wherever there are shoots which have single, pointed growth buds rather than more rounded, larger flower-buds, the single growth buds can be pinched out. Don't worry if you find it hard to distinguish between flower and growth buds; the best time to pinch is at or just after flowering, as the growth buds are expanding. At this time the buds are soft and easy to break off. If there are already two or more growth buds, leave these alone, only removing the single, central ones.

This practice is recommended for most larger rhododendrons until they reach flowering size. The exception to this is rhododendron species such as *R. arboreum*, *R. sinogrande*, *R. falconeri* and their relations, which have a natural tree-like habit, and which are at their best with a single tall trunk. Deciduous azaleas can be pruned before they come into growth or, to avoid losing the flowers, pinched after flowering, as the new growth elongates. Pinching is carried out methodically by nurserymen, and yet much rhododendron literature ignores this technique. If a little time is spent pinching your rhododendrons at the same time as deadheading them, more shapely plants will result.

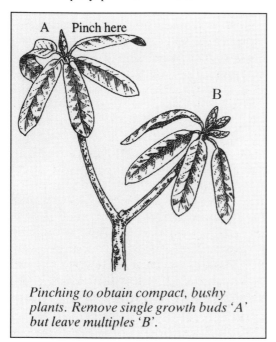

Pinching to obtain compact, bushy plants. Remove single growth buds 'A' but leave multiples 'B'.

For small-leaved (lepidote) rhododendrons and azaleas, some grow with leaves in rosettes as described above, requiring pinching out at the central bud. Others produce leaves all the way up the stems, and so can be pruned at any point up and down the stem, to encourage branching. Species such as *R. yunnanense* and its relations, and hybrids such as 'Yellowhammer', 'Praecox', 'Blue Diamond', 'Arctic Tern' and others benefit from regular pruning as small plants. Don't bother

about being too careful over this job; you can just take a pair of shears or secateurs over them in early summer to improve their shape. As the plants mature and flower freely, they will no longer need such regular pruning, although they can be cut back if they get too tall or straggly.

□ DEADHEADING

Removing dead rhododendron flowers from bushes is a time-consuming but worthwhile chore. If a rhododendron has been pollinated by insects (which is very likely with most varieties), its energy will be put into producing unwanted and often unsightly seed pods rather than into growing and setting flower buds for the following year. Some varieties set so much seed that they barely put on any new growth at all if they aren't deadheaded, so only manage to flower in alternate years. It is impossible to deadhead everything. Concentrate on young or valuable

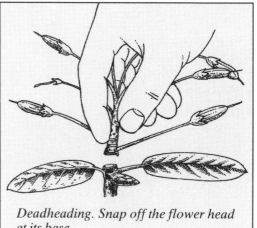

Deadheading. Snap off the flower head at its base.

plants, larger-leaved species, and plants which you want to grow the quickest.

Some dwarfs bear their flowers on stalks above the foliage, and their seeds can easily be cut off with a pair of scissors. For most other species and hybrids, the task of deadheading involves breaking the flower head off at the rosette of leaves below it. Be careful not to break off the expanding growth buds which surround the base of the truss. Deadheading can be a sticky job, as many species and hybrids have a glue-like covering on the flower stalk.

PESTS, DISEASES AND DISORDERS

□ PESTS

Fortunately there are few serious pests of rhododendrons, and only large collections generally suffer much from them. Bear in mind that insecticides kill all insects, including benign ones such as ladybirds, and many of them also affect birds, frogs and other members of the food chain. If your insects do only occasional damage, it is really not worth spraying them.

APHIDS

Small green or white insects which suck the sap out of leaves, particularly late in the growing season, causing a distorted shrivelled appearance. The most environmentally friendly sprays are soft soap, liquid derris or permethrin. The former is harmless to ladybirds and to other natural predators or aphids.

BIRDS

Birds tend to root up small plants looking for worms, etc, especially in very dry weather, when obviously plants which have their roots uncovered are vulnerable to damage from drying out. Netting or noisy bird-scarers seem to be the best option. The nectar of some flowers (especially waxy, red ones) is attractive to birds, and in getting it they sometimes tear up the flowers. Live and let live!

CATERPILLARS

Not usually a problem, but we find that some varieties seem to be attacked as the new growth unfurls. Caterpillars do not cut notches in the leaf margins (it is usually weevils, *q.v.*, which do this), but eat whole leaves or parts of leaves. Organic controls include picking off the caterpillars by hand, derris and pyrethrum. As the caterpillars usually drop out of nearby trees, moving the plant often solves the problem.

LACEBUGS

Adults and nymphs, 4mm (³⁄₁₆in) long, brownish-black insects with lace-like wings, suck sap from leaf undersides, causing brown discoloration on leaf undersides and yellow mottling above. Usually worst in full sun. Try pyrethrum, HCH or malathion.

MAMMALS

Rabbits and deer love certain rhododendrons, although unfortunately not *R. ponticum*! Deciduous and evergreen azaleas are particularly vulnerable. Rabbits and deer seem to be especially partial to plants which are precious, rare or small! Fencing or netting is the most usual response. Bags of human hair are supposed to deter deer from eating the plants they are hung on. A liquid chalk mixture is also available to spray on plants to make them taste bad to deer. While on the subject of mammals, don't let dogs and humans (especially with cameras) walk on your beds, as they compress the ground and usually break things. Provide stepping stones (or death threats!) if necessary.

WEEVILS
The most severe insect pest. The adult, dull black beetles make irregular notches in leaves, while the larvae feed on roots and stems, especially in containers, and can girdle the bark just below soil level, killing young plants. Weevils are very prevalent in some climates, and a preventive spraying programme is necessary. Many chemicals used to attack the larvae have been taken off the market in some countries. Orthene (U.S.A.) and HCH can be used to control adults. Larvae can be controlled by drenching the soil with permethrin. Some rhododendrons produce chemicals which appear to be natural weevil repellants. Perhaps in the future these will be synthesized as an organic control.

WHITEFLY
Tiny, white, moth-like insects whose pale-coloured scale-like young suck sap, usually during midsummer, causing yellowing of foliage, and excreting a sticky substance called honeydew which turns

---

□ QUICK GUIDE TO RHODODENDRON PROBLEMS

symptom	problem
Burned foliage	fertilizer damage (p.108) frost damage (p.110)
Chlorosis (yellow leaves)	lack of fertilizer/ minerals soil too alkaline/ wet/dry
Distorted foliage	aphids (summer) (p.102) spring frosts (p.110)
Flower buds lost	frosted (p.110)
Flower buds covered with black bristles	bud blast (p.104)
No flower buds formed	too much shade too much fertilizer (p.108) species/hybrid is shy flowering
Notches or holes in leaves	weevils (p.103) caterpillars (p.102)
Leaves: yellow above/ grey-brown below	powdery mildew (p.105)
black spotting	leaf spot (p.104)
yellow mottlings	lacebugs (p.102)
rusty patches below	rust (p.107)
black patches of sticky substance	whitefly (p.103)
Sudden death	frost damage/ bark split (p.108/110) honey fungus (p.104) root rot/wilt (p.107) weevils (p.103)

black and sooty. Remove by spraying leaf undersides with pyrethrum or permethrin.

□ DISEASES

BUD BLAST

In America, bud-blast refers to frosted buds, but in the U.K. and Europe it refers to a fungal disease. Black bristles cover the flower buds, causing them to dry up. Affects only certain varieties, particularly *R. caucasicum* and *R. ponticum*, and their hybrids such as 'Christmas Cheer'. Usually only some buds are affected. Not much can be done about it apart from picking off and burning the buds.

GALLS

Ugly green, pink, white or red swellings generally found at the ends of leaves. Common on evergreen azaleas and on *R. ferrugineum* and *R. hirsutum* and their hybrids. Pick off and burn. As a preventive spray, copper fungicide can be applied monthly from when growth starts.

HONEY FUNGUS (ARMILLARIA)

A fungus which normally lives on rotting wood and tree-stumps, particularly those of broad-leaved (hardwood) trees. It attacks the roots of rhododendrons, which can die slowly or suddenly. Long strands of brown or black rhizomorphs (root-like fungal tissue) can usually be found in the ground, and these sometimes produce yellow-brown toadstools in late summer. It is worst in wetter gardens, and at Glendoick we find the worst attacks occur during wet summers. Newly planted or otherwise stressed plants, in soggy soil for instance, seem to be the most susceptible. Very hard to eradicate; the best approach is to remove tree-stumps if possible. Stumps can be killed by drilling holes and filling them with diesel (diesel is very poisonous to all plants, so be careful). Alternatively, try to sterilize the soil and stump with a phenolic fungicide, but don't use this near rhododendron roots. New controls for honey fungus are being tested at the time of writing, but these have not yet reached the market.

LEAF SPOT

Black or brown spotting on the leaves. Some varieties such as 'Mrs G. W. Leak' have a genetic leaf-spot tendency. Leaf spot tends to affect other varieties if conditions are too damp or shaded. Fungicides such as benomyl or mancozeb should be able to help in severe cases, but usually moving the plant or reducing the shade will improve matters. Don't worry if some varieties show occasional leaf spotting, it is usually harmless.

LICHEN

Not a disease, and not harmful in itself, it is really a sign of an unhappy plant. It tends to cover stems of plants which are not in best health or vigour, especially on old, sparse, straggly evergreen and deciduous azaleas. If you can improve the vigour by pruning, fertilizer, transplanting, mulching, etc., the lichen will probably disappear.

Powdery mildew, showing typical patches of infection on the leaf underside.

PETAL BLIGHT
Brown or watery spots on petals, spreading over the entire flower, which quickly becomes brown and slimy. Rare outdoors in the U.K., but does affect flowers indoors in damp and humid conditions. In humid climates such as south-east U.S.A. and parts of Australia and New Zealand, this fungal disease can ruin flowers. Avoid overhead watering when plants are in flower, and if you expect trouble, spray the flowers with benomyl or mancozeb.

POWDERY MILDEW
This is a disease which rather suddenly started to attack rhododendrons in the U.K. in the early 1980s, and which has now spread to most milder parts of the rhododendron world. It remains to be seen if it will also attack rhododendrons in cold climates where winter lows regularly hit −18°C (0°F). In milder and moderate climates, it is undoubtedly the most serious disorder to affect rhododendrons. No one yet knows whether the mildew was introduced from another country, or whether it is a new mutation occurring spontaneously (or it may in fact be several related strains). Whatever its source, it has caused

severe damage in many of the finest rhododendron collections in the U.K., and has started to damage collections elsewhere.

The first symptoms are light green or yellowish rings on the upper leaf surface. In a short time, these rings are manifest on the leaf underside as spots or patches of whitish powder. These patches deepen to grey, black, brown or fawn, and in severe cases the whole of the lower leaf surface is covered, often causing the leaf to drop off. A defoliated bush may recover, but will sometimes be completely killed. Infection can appear soon after the new growth unfurls, and spraying should start at this time. In the mildest and wettest gardens it may be advisable to start spraying before this. Infection can appear at any time through the growing season, and spraying should be carried out every few weeks.

The species and hybrids in the following list will often be the first rhododendrons in a collection to show symptoms, but the disease will generally spread to others if it is not controlled. The list of species and hybrids in Chapter 3 includes references to these most susceptible varieties, and if you don't want to have to use fungicides on your rhododendrons, these otherwise very fine varieties should be avoided. So far, azaleas seem to be more or less resistant to powdery mildew, although there is a different type of mildew in the U.S.A. which affects deciduous azaleas.

There is at present no curative spray available for the disease, and only a preventive programme has any effect.

□ **VARIETIES MOST SUSCEPTIBLE TO POWDERY MILDEW**

R. cinnabarinum
R. succothii
R. thomsonii
'Anna Rose Whitney'
'Elizabeth'
'Lady Chamberlain'
'Lady Rosebery'
'Naomi'
'Seta'
'Virginia Richards'
+ hybrids of the above

Others quite susceptible include *R. barbatum*, *R. rubiginosum*, 'Bo Peep', 'Cynthia', 'Goldsworth Orange', 'Purple Splendour', 'Seven Stars', 'Whisperingrose' and many others.

Regular spraying of susceptible varieties throughout the growing period with fungicides such as benomyl, bupirimate and triforine, carbendazim, or thiophanate-methyl should provide some control. Fungicides available to the public are constantly being changed due to pesticide regulations, and to a certain extent, trial and error is the only course to follow. Use at least two unrelated fungicides in rotation to avoid a build up of resistance. It has recently been suggested that a systemic fungicide (which goes inside the leaf) should be alternated with a non-systemic one (which coats the leaf, preventing infection entering).

Bear in mind that the disease appears to enter the leaf underside, so spray must be applied from below, requiring a pressure sprayer of some type. For small gardens, very cheap hand pump sprayers are available which should be adequate. Knapsack sprayers are ideal for medium-sized collections, but larger ones will probably need some form of motor-driven sprayer. Wettest and mildest climates seem to suffer the worst from the disease, and unfortunately these climates also grow the largest rhododendrons, requiring the most spray.

At Glendoick we have found that the shadiest and most sheltered spots suffer the worst infections; in such areas a badly infected bush can easily infect most of its neighbours, even if they are normally resistant to the disease. Thinning out the rhododendrons or removing some shade and shelter has a beneficial effect, but of course a balance between adequate wind shelter and reduction of mildew-breeding conditions has to be maintained.

In a large collection, it is probably worth destroying the worst affected bushes to prevent infection of others. This may well mean the virtual disappearance of some species and hybrids from gardens in some areas, but this would be a necessary evil if it reduced overall infection. Hopefully over the next few years research will increase our knowledge of this disease, and some better preventive and curative sprays will be developed for the control of this most worrying affliction.

Will every rhododendron garden suffer from this disease? It is hard to say at present, but it seems that the more rhododendrons you have, the more rhododendrons there are in your neighbourhood, the milder your climate and the more shade and shelter you have, the more likely you are to find infection on your plants.

ROOT ROT/WILT (PHYTOPHTHORA)

A lethal disease which is most common in areas of high temperature and abundant moisture. Poor drainage and excess water are the usual causes of infection. Ideal conditions for its spread can arise in containers in cooler areas. It attacks the roots, and the plant slowly or suddenly wilts, collapses and dies. To ascertain if root rot was the cause of death, cut into the bark at soil level. Root rot causes the bark and central core of the stem to turn brown. The speed of the attack of this disease is also one of its characteristics. Whole plants or sections of them tend to wilt suddenly with no apparent cause. Root rot is unlikely to occur in garden conditions in the u.k., but it is a widespread problem in warmer climates. For container growing, ensure that drainage is good, by incorporating bark in the mixture, by avoiding black pots (which heat up), and by preventing waterlogging in any part of the container. Some fungicides do control root rot; try Metalxyl, Prothiocarb or Etridiazole (not u.k.), but once the symptoms appear, there is nothing you can do to save a plant.

RUST

A fungal disease which causes orange

patches to appear on the leaf underside of certain varieties. It spreads on the new growth, especially in warm and humid conditions. Several different strains exist. It commonly attacks hybrids such as 'Lady Alice Fitzwilliam' and 'Fragrantissimum' (particularly if grown indoors), some *R. cinnabarinum* hybrids and several dwarf hybrids. The affected leaves should be removed and burned (they will soon fall off anyway). A fungicide containing bupirimate/triforine works effectively as a preventive spray.

☐ OTHER DISORDERS

BARK SPLIT
The plant equivalent of burst water pipes after frost; the stem freezes, causing the bark to split open. Caused by frosts while sap is running in the plant, either in autumn or more commonly in the spring after growth has begun. At the time of writing, we are experiencing a very mild winter, bringing plants into growth two months earlier than usual, making them very vulnerable to bark split from the inevitable spring frosts. Branches where the bark has split may heal, but often gradual deterioration will take place, with yellowing leaves and weak growth. In such cases, pruning is usually advisable. A really severe frost can cause so much damage, especially on a small plant, that the whole plant can be killed outright. Several species and hybrids tend to grow early, becoming particularly vulnerable. *R. williamsianum* and its hybrids are commonly grown examples. Plants can be protected with sacking, blankets, branches and other materials, or you can just avoid planting early growing plants if you live in an area of severe spring frosts. Such plants are indicated in the descriptions in Chapter 3 (see also Frost Damage, p.110).

CHLOROSIS
Yellowing of the leaves, or patches of yellow between the veins on the leaves. Usually caused by soil problems such as alkaline soil, excess water, overdeep planting, insect damage, lack of fertilizer or mineral deficiency. If the soil is well-drained, acid and fertilized, and the plants are correctly planted, the chlorosis will probably be due to a mineral deficiency such as lack of iron or magnesium. It may be worth identifying your missing mineral by having your soil analysed, as large additions of unnecessary minerals can cause more damage than good to rhododendrons (see also p.88-92).

FERTILIZER BURN
Usually brown, burned patches at the ends or edges of the leaves. Certain varieties resent fertilizer and should generally not be fed at all. Always apply fertilizer in small quantities two to three times per season, rather than in one large dose, and ensure that your fertilizer is not a nitrate-based one, which releases large quantities of nitrogen too quickly (see p.92).

(Opposite), *Knaphill and Exbury azaleas provide a riot of colour in late spring, particularly in orange and yellow shades.*

FROST DAMAGE

The most common frost damage is of flowers and flower buds. In most areas early flowering rhododendrons are at risk of having their flowers frosted, and there are only a few varieties whose flowers can sail unscathed through frost. Many varieties such as *R.* 'Cilpinense' and *R.* 'Snow Lady' have buds which are frost-tender as soon as they start to swell. Artificial protection can see flowers through several degrees of frost.

Winter damage to foliage can be caused by winds, sun, frost or a combination of all three. Whole leaves or just patches on them become brittle and dried, grey or brown. A variety which is damaged may be just too tender for the site it is in; moving it to a more favourable situation, or giving artificial protection, will help. The worst winter damage is often caused by the combination of frost and sun, producing rapid freezing and thawing, or causing the leaves to lose moisture in the sun, while the ground is frozen, preventing water being taken up. The effect is compounded by winds. The frost-sun combination causes the leaves to curl up or wilt; this is usually not serious for very short periods, but can be fatal if prolonged.

Shelter, light shade or only part-day sun will usually prevent this type of damage. If this is impossible, artificial protection similar to that used for spring frosts can be used on more tender varieties. Whatever shelter is used, ensure that ventilation is maintained to prevent overheating, and don't leave soggy materials lying over foliage for long periods, as this causes mould and rotting.

Probably the most common frost damage, which can be suffered by even the hardiest varieties, is distorted new growth caused by late frosts after the growth buds have started to elongate. This is a common problem in the U.K., due to the unpredictability of the weather. If the weather is mild in early spring, plants invariably start growing before frost danger has passed. Some varieties commonly make early growth; these will often need artificial protection in the spring.

Cloches, sacking, conifer branches, cardboard boxes, newspaper and many other materials will usually provide sufficient protection from several degrees of frost. Water soluble materials lose much of their frost-protection ability when wet, so such materials will need to be regularly taken off and returned. Polythene really only helps if it is not touching the plant itself; it should be supported on a frame. As with bark split (see p.108), small plants will suffer the most damage, and so need the most protection.

If your plants have been frosted, the growth will unfurl short, shrivelled and distorted, or it can be completely burned off. If damaged growth is pruned off, new shoots will usually sprout. If your garden has an extensive sprinkler system, you can use this to prevent damage from several degrees of spring frost. Turn on the sprinklers when the temperature drops to freezing, and the air circulation which results will keep the local temperature above freezing. Obviously this tends to flood the

'Panda', a Glendoick Japanese azalea hybrid, ideal for cooler and more northerly climates.

garden and can lead to large water bills.

ROLLED LEAVES
A natural response to cold or dry conditions. When the cells in the leaves dry out, they contract, causing the leaves to curl or wilt. This helps to conserve moisture by reducing the surface area available for evaporation. It will only cause lasting damage if freez-ing or drought is severe (see Frost Damage, described earlier).

SUNBURN
Yellow patches on the leaves, some-times with brown, burned areas. If a bush with brown or yellow leaves is unaffected on its lower leaves and/or on its shadier side, then sun is probably the problem. Move to a shadier site.

CHAPTER FIVE

PROPAGATION

Rhododendrons can be propagated either vegetatively or by seed. Vegetative propagation involves producing a new plant from a shoot of the parent plant, usually by layers or cuttings. Alternatively the shoot can be grafted on to a rootstock. A vegetatively propagated plant is genetically identical to the parent, and all named hybrids and clones of species must be produced this way. Propagation from seed, even if careful pollination between two species is carried out, results in all the seedlings being unique plants, which may be similar to the parents but which are NOT genetically identical.

LAYERING

This is the easiest way for the amateur to propagate a few extra plants vegetatively. Theoretically this technique can be successfully used for all varieties. Layering involves bending down a shoot (or shoots) to the ground where it is anchored, using stones or pegs, until the shoot produces its own roots. This can generally be done at any time of the year.

Layering, showing a branch pegged into the soil with the end of the shoot positioned upwards.

The soil used to root the bent shoot usually needs to be prepared by adding organic matter, and the shoot should be bent into as upright a position as possible. Attach the shoot to a stake to achieve this if necessary. Growth from the previous year or two is generally the most successful. For dwarf types, use the current year's growth in late summer as soon as it is hard enough to bend without breaking. To encourage rooting, larger growers with thick shoots should usually have a layer of bark removed from the bottom of the shoot where it is buried. Layers should be carefully watered during dry periods.

It usually takes one to three years for the shoot to produce sufficient roots to be able to grow independently of the parent. It can then be severed from the mother plant. The layer can be moved immediately, but it is safer to leave it for a season's growth, as the double shock of severing and transplanting can be fatal. An alternative is to layer into boxes or pots (which can be plunged into the soil), so allowing the layer to be removed after severing without disturbing the roots. Not surprisingly, most layers have a bend at the bottom and judicious pruning may have to be done to get a shapely plant (see p.98).

Several shoots may be layered off a bush at one time, and although it may look like unacceptable cruelty, a whole plant can in fact be layered. The rootball can be placed on its side to allow the branches to be pegged into the soil. Multiple layering is especially easy with dwarf types with low, thin, supple branches. Layers generally need a fair amount of mollycoddling for their first few seasons after being severed, and particular attention should be paid to keeping them well watered during the summer.

CUTTINGS

Relative to many other common garden shrubs, most rhododendron cuttings are quite hard and slow to root without heated propagation facilities. Despite this, there are some varieties which can be successfully rooted without heat in a cold frame, or even on a windowsill in a homemade propagator. The easiest include most evergreen azaleas, some dwarf species and hybrids including dwarf purple-blues such as *R. fastigiatum* and *R.* 'Blue Diamond', the dwarf reds such as *R.* 'Scarlet Wonder' and other hybrids such as *R.* 'Curlew' and *R.* 'Pink Drift'.

Cuttings need a well-drained medium, and protection from direct sunlight, but must never be allowed to dry out. Use a container which is at least 5 cm (2 in) deep (deeper for large varieties) and which has plenty of drainage holes at the bottom. A cold frame, deep seed trays, boxes, garden pots and saucers and old food containers can be used. There are many formulae for rooting mediums; the one we use at Glendoick contains 50% peat and 50% bark or acid sharp sand (both by volume).

Cuttings should usually be taken from the current year's growth in late summer and early autumn, and it keeps the parent plant tidy if the cutting is removed right down to the next circle of leaves. Dwarfs and some species root best if taken fairly early in the summer, as soon as the stems are hard enough, while most hardy hybrids root best taken in the autumn and even in midwinter. One way to tell whether cuttings are ripe enough is that it should be possible to bend them almost double without breaking them. Cuttings which are taken too soft rot off very quickly.

Keep cuttings cool and in polythene bags until they can be planted. Dwarf cuttings should be 2.5–5 cm (1–2 in) long; larger varieties can be longer. The lower leaves should be removed, leaving three to five leaves at the top of the shoot, and large flower buds should generally be taken out. Thicker-stemmed varieties can have a shallow wound sliced into the bark, on one or both sides of the stems; it should start from the base of the cutting and be as long as the depth the cutting is pushed into the soil. Varieties with large leaves can have the end of the leaves cut to save space. Dipping the cuttings in hormone rooting powders or liquids increases the speed of rooting.

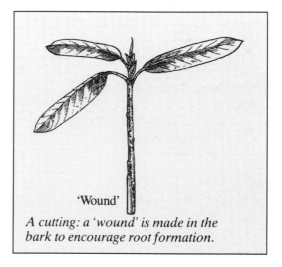

'Wound'

A cutting: a 'wound' is made in the bark to encourage root formation.

Although small-scale mist systems are available, the amount of moisture they produce is hard to control correctly, and I would recommend instead, covering the cuttings with polythene, usually laid directly on top of them, anchored at the sides to prevent air entering and drying out the leaves. If you use individual pots and other containers, put several cuttings in each and use a polythene bag to obtain an airtight environment. Under polythene, water will condense on the inside, ensuring a permanently humid environment. Spots where there is no condensation indicate dryness or air getting in under the polythene. Don't push cuttings too far into the rooting medium; half their length or less is sufficient, unless the cuttings are very short, and be careful not to overfirm the medium. Cuttings can be placed close together, but avoid overlapping leaves, as the lower ones will tend to rot off. Place the cuttings in a bright situation but shaded from direct sunlight. They should be regularly checked, and rotted cuttings and dead leaves should be removed. Don't allow them to dry out at any stage, but it is most important to avoid overwatering.

Speed of rooting and likelihood of success with harder-to-root types is increased by the use of artificial heat. Electric propagators are widely available for this purpose, or alternatively lengths of heating cables can be purchased from garden centres. The temperature should be kept around 18–21°C (65–70°F) during the summer and autumn, but should be gradually turned down to 10°C (50°F) during the winter when light levels are low.

Cuttings can take anything from six weeks to nine months to root, and some varieties will rarely root at all. The beginner should probably try evergreen azaleas first, and then move on to harder varieties. When the cuttings have rooted, they should be gradually hardened off by slitting the polythene. Transplant the cuttings into a lime-free, peat-based compost when they start into growth. Several manufacturers make an ericaceous compost which is ideal for this purpose. Alternatively, a home-made compost can consist of a mixture of approximately 60% by volume of peat, and 40% bark, preferably with some leafmould or conifer needles included. Liquid fertilizers can be used, but watch out for leaf scorch if the fertilizer is too concentrated. Several weak applications are preferable to one strong one. Cuttings can be planted outside once they have made their first growth, but they are best moved to a 'nursery' area for a year or two, where they can be more carefully looked after.

For deciduous azaleas and deciduous rhododendrons such as *R. dauricum* and *R. mucronulatum*, softwood cuttings provide the best results. These are taken about a month after the new growth first appears. Use weak rooting hormones to avoid scorching. In colder areas the stock plants are often brought inside so that they come into growth earlier.

GRAFTING

A technique for the adventurous, used to propagate larger species and hybrids when a shoot (called a scion) is fitted over and on to a rootstock. For the graft to be successful the cambium layers (just below the bark) of the scion and rootstock must callus and fuse together. When this fusion is complete, the plant is able to move liquids up and down the stem from the rootstock to the scion, allowing the scion to grow.

In the U.K., America, Australia and New Zealand, grafting is generally only used to propagate varieties which are hard or impossible to root from cuttings. In northern Europe, grafting is the standard technique used for rhododendron production. The reason for this is that a rootstock such as 'Cunningham's White' manages to impart beneficial characteristics to the variety grafted on top. These include greater vigour, more compact plants, greener foliage, faster budding and greater all-round tolerance of the climate there. For the amateur in West Germany, Denmark, Sweden, Switzerland, Norway, Holland and countries of similar climate, grafting can be recommended for all elepidote hybrids and species. In other countries, it is probably only worth grafting harder-to-root varieties. Lepidote (smaller, scaly-leaved) rhododendrons and evergreen azaleas are not grafted.

Rootstocks can be obtained in several ways. Easy-to-root varieties such as *R.* 'Cunningham's White' are rooted from cuttings and grown on for one to two years before being used. In some areas these can be bought ready for grafting. Alternatively, surplus seedlings of two to three years of age can be used. Species such as *R. decorum*, *R. vernicosum*, *R. calophytum* and others are all successful. Do not use *R. ponticum*, unless it is the only stock available, as it nearly always produces masses of suckers which must constantly be removed, and in addition, it is very susceptible to

root rot (phytophthora, see p.107) in hotter and humid climates. Choose a stock which is as hardy or hardier than the scion to be grafted on to it, and match rootstocks to scions of plants of roughly similar size and vigour. Most importantly, the scion must have a similar stem diameter to that of the rootstock. Rootstocks should be partially dried out four to six weeks before grafting. Many people grow rootstocks in containers which are brought inside in the autumn to dry out.

Although grafting can be done at any time of year, there are two periods which are most commonly used. In late summer, 'green' grafting is practised. This has the advantage of not requiring heat and is probably the best time of year for the amateur. Side grafts (see below) are generally used at this time of year. The other common grafting period is during mid- and late winter. Winter grafting usually requires bottom heat of 15–18°C (59–65°F) or so.

For all grafting, a scion (shoot) 4–5 cm (1½–2 in) long, just like a cutting, is selected. There are several different types of graft, each favoured by different people. Two of the most popular are those called a saddle graft and a side graft. The most important tool for either is a very sharp knife. For a saddle graft, the rootstock is pruned, leaving a single stem 4–10 cm (1½–4 in) in length from the rootball, and all leaves are removed. All growth buds should be rubbed off. The rootstock then has two cuts, approximately 2.5 cm (1 in) long, made into the top of the stem, giving a screwdriver-head shape. The basal end of the

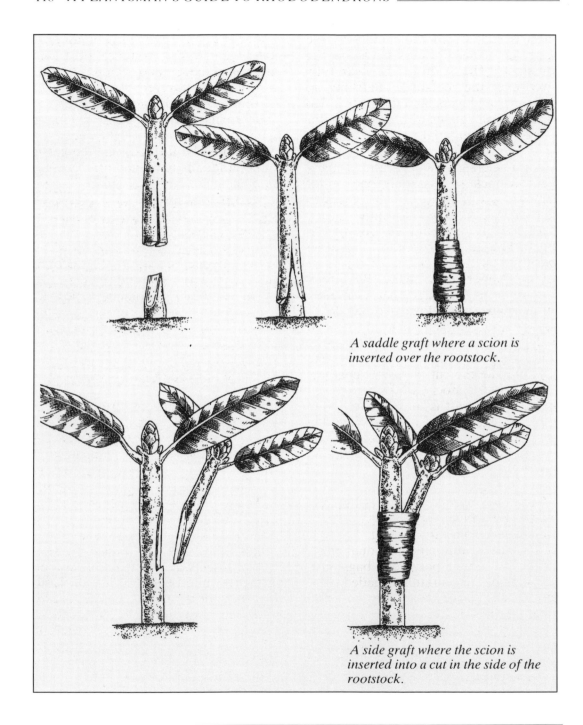

A saddle graft where a scion is inserted over the rootstock.

A side graft where the scion is inserted into a cut in the side of the rootstock.

scion is split down the middle to the same length as the cuts made on the rootstock. The scion is then carefully fitted over the rootstock, matching up the cambium layers, and the graft is tied in place with rubber ties, tape, raffia or other similar material.

For a side (or veneer) graft, cut back the rootstock so that only one set of leaves is left. These can then be cut to save space. A slice of around 2.5 cm (1 in) long is made in the side of the rootstock. Do not cut into more than one third of the thickness of the rootstock; deeper cuts make the stock vulnerable to breakage. Another short cut is made at a downward angle to remove the thin flap, leaving a small shelf for the scion to sit on. For a side graft, the scion should be cut on one side, making the cut the same length as the one on the stock, so that it fits into the cut. The graft is then carefully tied in place. Some people like to leave the flap in place and in this case, the screwdriver-head-shaped scion should be used.

Once the grafts have been made, they must be put into an airtight environment and shaded from direct sunlight. If you green-graft in autumn, individual grafts can be put under polythene bags on a north-facing or carefully shaded windowsill. For larger quantities, a small covering structure or frame is usually used. A propagator is quite good, but it may be too shallow for larger varieties. One easy method is to use a deep seed tray or propagator base. The grafts are

packed in tightly, planted in an approximately 50:50 (by volume) peat and bark/sand mixture and watered lightly. They are then covered completely with polythene. As with cuttings, water will condense inside the polythene as long as it is airtight. In four to eight weeks the union should be formed, and the grafts can be gradually hardened off. Turn off the heat and ensure the grafts are not allowed to dry out. Keep a graft well protected for its first growing season. Grafting is considered by some to be an art-form or a God-given gift, too difficult for anyone but experts to perform. This really is not so, and good results are quite easily achieved, especially from autumn (green) grafting. See the further reading list on p.125 for more information.

SEED

Raising rhododendrons from seed is harder than raising most flower and vegetable seeds, but with a little care it can be very successful. Rhododendrons produce copious amounts of seed, but they also hybridize so easily that any seed picked off a bush which has not been isolated from other rhododendrons flowering at the same time will probably have been hybridized by bees or other insects. Because of this, obtaining worthwhile seed can be difficult. Most rhododendron societies have seed-exchange programmes where seed of specially made hybrids and carefully pollinated species can be obtained by members (you don't have to have your own seed to exchange). The most exciting seed to raise is that collected in the wild. If you cannot collect it yourself, it is often possible to subscribe to seed from a collecting trip, or to obtain it from a rhododendron society seed exchange. Always record the collector's number on wild seed.

To get viable seed from hand pollinated species, you generally require more than one clone; rhododendrons are generally not self-fertile. Although very many rhododendrons can be hybridized with one another, the smaller leaved, scaly leaved types cannot be crossed with the larger leaved ones. Likewise, rhododendrons generally cannot be crossed with azaleas. Apart from these barriers, and one or two others caused by differing chromosome counts, most rhododendrons can be crossed with one another, although not every pollination will succeed due to weather and other factors. Pollinations which are frosted in the spring will not set seed. Pollen can be stored for several weeks in the refrigerator to allow crosses to be made between plants which flower at different times.

To obtain good seed from your own rhododendrons, it is important that only deliberate pollination takes place; insects must be prevented from assisting you, or the results will be disappointing. It takes a minimum of four years (and often much longer) to see the flowers of most rhododendrons grown from seed, so take great care to avoid contaminated or open-pollinated seed. To hand pollinate seed, it is important to prepare a flower before it opens. Select the plant to be used as the female (seed-bearing) parent. Just before the flower bud opens, remove the petals and the stamens, leaving only the stigma, so that the flower is made uninteresting to insects. The stigma usually needs to be left for a few days to become sticky, so label the prepared flower so that you can find it again. After a few days, pollen from another plant's stamens can be applied. The more flowers you prepare for each pollination, the better chance you have of getting good seed.

Carefully label and record the pollination so that you can find it again later. The seed capsules ripen in autumn, turning brown and eventually splitting, emptying their contents. Dwarfs tend to ripen the earliest, while late-flowering larger species and hybrids often will not ripen until midwinter. Seed should be collected just before splitting, when the capsules have turned from green to brown. Even if the capsules have split before you collect it, there is usually some seed inside which can be shaken out. Rhododendron seed is very small, ranging from dust-like to irregular flattish shapes 2mm ($\frac{1}{10}$in) in diameter. The seeds should be shaken from their capsules and cleaned of as much chaff as possible. They can be stored for quite long periods in a refrigerator, and can easily be sent through the mail, making seed the cheapest way to exchange rhododendron material.

Seed is usually sown in winter into clean pots of fine peat. Soak the peat by standing the pots in water, and never water small seeds overhead. Sprinkle seed thinly over the surface and cover with polythene or glass. At a tempera-

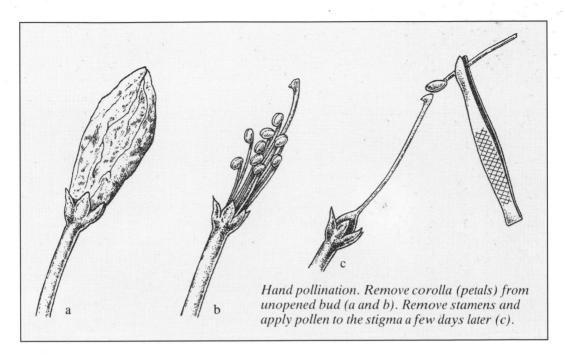

Hand pollination. Remove corolla (petals) from unopened bud (a and b). Remove stamens and apply pollen to the stigma a few days later (c).

ture of 18–20°C (65–68°F), germination takes only two to three weeks. If you have no heat, seed can be sown in a cool greenhouse or cold frame; germination can sometimes take several months. Seed pans should be put in a bright situation, but ensure that they are shaded from direct sunlight. Seed can be effectively raised under artificial lights; ordinary fluorescent striplights work well.

Never let seed pans dry out and only water them from below when the seedlings are small, to avoid rotting. Seedlings can be transplanted into boxes as soon as they are large enough, or left (if not overcrowded) for their first season. Dilute liquid feed can be used to speed up growth. Many seedlings grow very slowly and this method of propagation is undoubtedly for the patient!

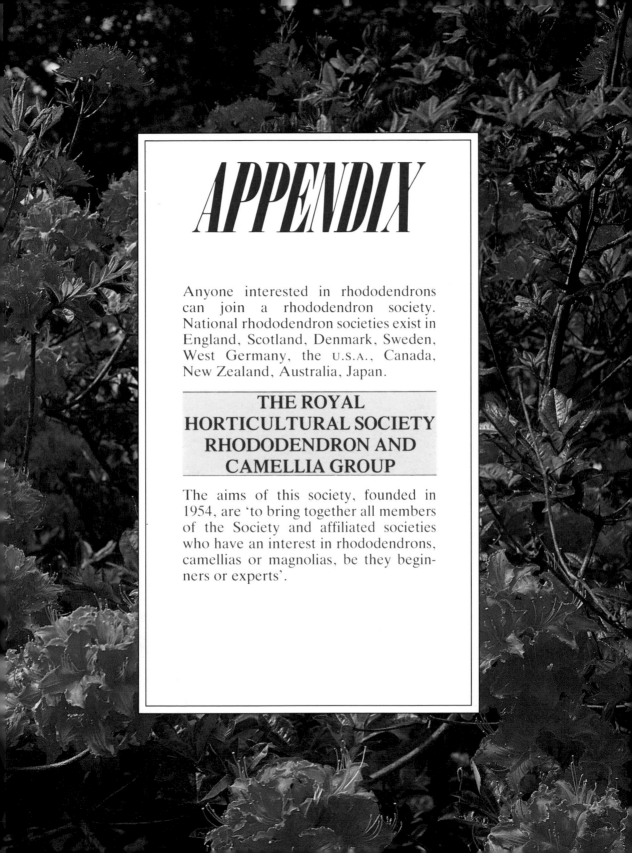

APPENDIX

Anyone interested in rhododendrons can join a rhododendron society. National rhododendron societies exist in England, Scotland, Denmark, Sweden, West Germany, the U.S.A., Canada, New Zealand, Australia, Japan.

THE ROYAL HORTICULTURAL SOCIETY RHODODENDRON AND CAMELLIA GROUP

The aims of this society, founded in 1954, are 'to bring together all members of the Society and affiliated societies who have an interest in rhododendrons, camellias or magnolias, be they beginners or experts'.

The Group currently has more than 600 members, most of them in the u.k. and Ireland, but with others in most rhododendron-growing countries. Each year, the Group publishes a Yearbook which contains articles on plant collecting expeditions, fine rhododendron gardens, cultivation advice, show and award reports and other information. Published in conjunction with the year book is a supplement to the 1958 *International Rhododendron Register* describing all the new hybrids and species clonal selections registered during the previous year. A four-monthly bulletin is also published containing information on the activities of the various local branches of the society. These branches include South East, South West (England), South West Wales, East Anglia and Ireland. Each of these branches organizes its own local activities which may include, among other things, garden visits and lectures.

The main Group organizes a yearly tour in some part of the United Kingdom (normally of about seven days' duration), and also a one day outing and social gathering over a weekend in mid autumn. Members compete at two shows in London at the Royal Horticultural Society's Halls in Vincent Square. The first takes place in early spring, and the main show in the first week of May. All members of the society are encouraged to exhibit in the many classes.

The annual subscription is currently a reasonable £7, which includes the Yearbook and bulletins. The Group can be contacted through their secretary, Ray Redford, Fairbank, 39 Rectory Road, Farnborough, Hants GU14 7BT, u.k.

THE AMERICAN RHODODENDRON SOCIETY

Formed in 1945 in Oregon, u.s.a. In 1951 other chapters (branches) were formed in New York, Seattle, Eugene, San Francisco and Richmond. Since then chapters have been started all over the u.s.a., and also in western Canada, Denmark and Scotland.

The aims of the society are: 'to encourage interest in and to disseminate knowledge about rhododendrons and azaleas, and provide a medium through which all persons interested in rhododendrons and azaleas may communicate and cooperate with others through education, meetings, publications, scientific studies, research and other similar activities'.

The American Rhododendron Society has over 5000 members worldwide, and its various chapters are very active. Most chapters meet regularly, hold shows, garden visits, lectures, plant sales and auctions, book sales, etc. There are several gardens run by the society, maintaining collections of species and hybrids. In the u.s.a., frequent conferences lasting several days are held, where many of the leading growers and experts give lectures, hold discussions with members, and visit gardens. The American Rhododendron Society has its own award and rating system, a huge seed-exchange published in January/February each year, and it runs a research programme on all aspects of the genus. Members receive a quarterly colour journal with informative articles from all over the world on all aspects of rhododendron and azalea cultivation.

Dues are currently $20 per year, or $300 for life membership. The society can be contacted via Paula Cash, Executive Secretary, 14885 S.W. Sunrise Lane, Tigard, Oregon 97224, u.s.a.

THE SCOTTISH RHODODENDRON SOCIETY

The Scottish Chapter of the American Rhododendron Society was formed in 1983, largely through the energies of Mr Ed Wright of Arduaine Gardens in Argyllshire, Scotland. All the facilities of the parent society are available to members, and they receive the quarterly journal. The Scottish Rhododendron Society holds a yearly show and its Annual General Meeting in late spring. Spring and autumn meetings are held each year, when the fine Scottish rhododendron collections are visited, and members can socialize and share information. The Scottish Rhododendron Society can be contacted through Hubert Andrew, Stron Ailne, Colintrave, Argyll PA22 3AS.

FURTHER INFORMATION

There are many fine books and publications for further reading. The following includes some of the most useful; many other more specialized books are also available.

Cox, E.H.M. *Plant Hunting in China*, Collins 1945/Oxford, 1986.
Cox, P.A. *The Larger Species of Rhododendron*, Batsford, London, 1979/1989.
Cox, P.A. *The Smaller Rhododendrons*, Batsford, London, 1985.
Cox, P.A. and K.N.E. *The Encyclopedia of Rhododendron Hybrids*, Batsford, London, 1988.
Cox, P.A. and K.N.E. *The Cox Guide to Choosing Rhododendrons*, Batsford, London, 1990.
Fairweather, C. *Rhododendrons and Azaleas*, Floraprint, Nottingham, 1979 (new edition in preparation).
Leach, D.G. *Rhododendrons of the World*, Allen and Unwin, London, 1962.
Leslie, A. (compiler) *The Rhododendron Handbook 1980, Species in Cultivation*, Royal Horticultural Society, 1980.
Salley, H.E. and Greer, H.E. *Rhododendron Hybrids, A Guide to their Origins*, Timber Press, Oregon, 1986.
Street, J.F. *Azaleas*, Cassell, London, 1959.
Street, J. F. *Rhododendrons*, Cassell, London, 1965.

INDEX

This is a name only index containing first species and then hybrids of rhododendrons.

ACKNOWLEDGEMENTS

The publishers are grateful to the following for granting
permission to reproduce the colour photographs: the
Harry Smith Horticultural Photographic Collection
(pp. 8/9, 26, 27 and 41); Kenneth Cox (pp. 12, 14, 16,
18/19, 29, 35, 36, 39, 42/43, 45, 53, 55, 58, 65, 69, 73,
78, 80, 86/87, 89, 99, 105, 109, 111 and 112/113); Photos
Horticultural Picture Library (pp. 21, 23, 31, 61, 83 and
122/123). The photograph on pp. 112/113 was taken by
Bob Challinor.
All the line drawings were drawn by Nils Solberg.